The Techniques of Writing: Form A

The Techniques of Writing:

Form A

Paul L. Kinsella
Southeastern Campus, Indiana University

Harcourt, Brace & World, Inc.
New York / *Chicago* / *San Francisco* / *Atlanta*

ISBN: 0-15-589717-9

Library of Congress Catalog Card Number: 67-14188

Printed in the United States of America

A Note to the Instructor

This book stresses those basic principles that I believe students need to know if they are to write acceptably on the college level. It gives priority to the problems that harass a large percentage of college freshmen, as shown by errors and deficiencies in hundreds of their themes that I have graded over the past several years. And on the whole the presentation follows my strong conviction that it is better to teach a few principles thoroughly than many superficially.

I have tried throughout to emphasize writing as a branch of language closely related to speaking rather than as a highly technical and special form of communication. I am convinced that many college students, especially those who find writing difficult, have developed a psychological block. Many are confused by grammatical terms and definitions they do not understand. Many believe that writing is not related to speaking. Thus their diction is often unnatural, flowery, pretentious—but (even worse) vague, imprecise, and sometimes incomprehensible. I have urged the student to take advantage of his innate language ability as a way to overcome his fear of writing. The exercises in the lessons on inflated diction and deadwood, for example, give the student practice in detecting pretentious and imprecise writing, thus leading him toward a more concise and lucid style.

I have also strongly emphasized organization, for obviously many students find writing difficult because they do not know how to shape their thoughts— they do not really know what they are trying to say. For this reason, I have begun the book with a lesson on organizing the theme and have keyed the next two lessons as well to the outline. If a student can learn to organize his material, his writing is almost bound to improve. Often the improvement is remarkable, convincing me that learning to outline properly cannot be overly stressed.

Every instructor will use these lessons in his own way, but a few ideas based on my experience may be of interest. I believe that most students will learn more if all the lessons are covered at a fairly fast pace and reviewed periodically. Most of the exercises can be completed and usually discussed in a single class period.

The exercises on logic, deadwood, and inflated diction, however, will probably take an hour of a student's time and might be given as an out-of-class assignment to be discussed in class. An instructor wishing to stress spelling might assign fifty words each week, repeating the same procedure during the latter six weeks of the semester. In addition to the drills the instructor will probably wish to use the tests available for each lesson, and the true-false tests to check student understanding of the various principles.

The approach embodied here works well in my composition classes. I hope it may be helpful to other teachers and students as well.

Paul Kinsella

Jeffersonville, Indiana

Contents

Lesson 1

Organizing the Theme

Perhaps the most difficult step in writing is getting started. If you think seriously about how you think, you will realize that your mind usually flits from one idea to another. Hardly ever do your thoughts fall naturally into the pattern of a first-rate college theme, unless you make a definite effort to organize your general ideas and supporting facts. Many students write poorly because they do not organize their thoughts intelligently.

Topic Outline

Writing a theme is similar to building a house. Just as no experienced contractor would think of building a house without blueprints, a student should not attempt to write a theme without an outline. In both cases, much effort would probably be wasted on false starts and costly or time-consuming revisions. And still the end product would probably lack the symmetry and sharpness that come from careful planning. The introduction of the theme would be vague, the succeeding paragraphs disorganized, and the conclusion abrupt. A student writing a theme could also be likened to a person taking an auto trip: both should have a destination. Just as the driver must stay on the right road to reach his destination quickly and efficiently, the writer must also follow a plan (an outline) to reach his goal — the clear and precise communication of his ideas.

Perhaps the greatest barrier to effective planning is that many students think outlining is a waste of time and that if they could spell or learn grammar their writing problems would be solved. They do not realize that their basic need is to think clearly; the reason they cannot write effectively is that their thoughts are not organized. For such students an outline is the key to effective writing.

Scratch Outline

Although your thoughts may be jumbled, try jotting them down as they come to you. In this way they will flow freely, since you will not worry about spelling, sentence structure, or other such problems. If, for example, you are asked to write a short theme on "My Best High School Teacher" you can jot down your ideas in the form of a *scratch outline* just as they come to your mind. It might look like this:

> Coached the baseball team
> Sponsored the yearbook
> Pitched for the home town semipro team
> Graduated with honors from Indiana University
> Treated all students fairly
> Always willing to give students personal assistance
> Knew his subject thoroughly
> Spent a minimum of time lecturing
> Kept the students busy working on drills and themes
> Had the students write some of their themes in class
> Created interest in literature by using films and recordings
> Was active in community affairs
> Directed the community theater and often acted in the plays

After you have put down your ideas in grocery-list fashion, you are ready for the second step, that of converting the scratch outline into a topic outline. This is one of the most challenging and difficult steps in writing. For if you can formulate an intelligent topic outline you can learn to write a unified composition. As a matter of fact, after you have constructed a good topic outline, your theme is all but written. The important thing is to come up with main divisions and subtopics that are equal in value or rank and grammatically parallel.

What is meant by *equal in value or rank*? The same principle is frequently stated in more technical terms that you, as a composition student, should know: the main divisions as well as the subtopics of your outline should be *logically coordinate*. No doubt the best way to understand this fundamental principle is to study specific examples from outlines. Proper *coordination* is the key to successful outlining, and unless you understand it you will probably never be able to make a good outline and write a superior theme.

To achieve coordination decide on the main divisions before you worry about the subtopics. Such an approach will make it easier for you to form broad divisions that are similar in scope or importance and that will help you to write a well balanced theme. If the main parts of your outline are not coordinate (of equal value or rank), your theme will be lopsided and disorganized, and the reader will have difficulty following your line of thought. Make a special effort to understand this basic principle in outlining; it is the key to successful writing.

Now consider the following one-level outline and decide if it is coordinate.

MY BEST TEACHER   *ex of a level outline*

Introduction
I. At school
II. Away from school
Conclusion

It is apparent that the outline *is* coordinate, because the two main divisions are approximately equal in value or importance. But consider this outline:

MY BEST TEACHER

Introduction
I. At school
II. Pitched for semipro baseball team

This outline is *not* coordinate as you can readily see, because there is a logical difference between the two topics. *At school* designates a place while *pitched for semipro baseball team* points to an action.

Let us consider another example that illustrates the ability to distinguish between generalizations and facts, a skill that is necessary in writing an effective paragraph as well as a successful theme.

ADMIRABLE TRAITS

Introduction
I. Honesty
II. Ambition
III. Humor
Conclusion

Are these main divisions coordinate? Since honesty, ambition, and humor are distinct character traits that can be observed in a person's actions and speech and discussed at length by giving specific examples and illustrations, they can — for the purpose of writing a theme based on the title — be considered as coordinate. But suppose we alter the outline in this manner:

ADMIRABLE TRAITS

Introduction
I. Honesty
II. Attended night classes at the university
III. Humor
Conclusion

Our sense of order should tell us that something is wrong with the outline. Further thought should show that a fact (*Attended night classes at the University*) has been inserted between two generalizations. Although *Honesty* and *Humor* can be logically subdivided by moving from the general to the more specific, *Attended night classes at the university* cannot be divided in the same way. If you were writing a four-hundred-word theme based on the above outline, you would probably discover, after you finished your first draft, that the second topic (*Attended night classes at the university*) was covered in one short paragraph, while the other two main divisions required considerably more space. Thus we must conclude that the outline is not coordinate, because the second main division is not of the same value as *Honesty* and *Humor*.

What has been said of the main divisions also applies to the subtopics of an outline. Let us consider this three-level outline on the same subject.

ADMIRABLE TRAITS

Introduction
  I. Honesty
     A. With himself
        1. Did not rationalize his behavior
        2. Did not project his own faults onto others
     B. With others
 II. Ambition
     A. Business
        1. Stayed extra hours at office
        2. Took work home with him at night
     B. Civic affairs
III. Humor
     A. Laughed at his own failures
     B. Laughed with, not at, other people
Conclusion

The main divisions, you will recall, are coordinate. But what about the subtopics (*With himself* and *With others*) under the first main division? Placing them side by side and studying the structure of the language is one important test of coordination. You will notice that A and B both begin with the same preposition and that *himself* and *others* are pronouns—a good reason to suppose they are coordinate. But similarity in language does not mean the outline has passed the test. The writer still must carefully weigh the relative importance of the topics in relation to what he is trying to accomplish in his theme. In this instance it would appear that A (*With himself*) and B (*With others*) are coordinate.

Now let us move to the third level under IA. Are 1 (*Did not rationalize his behavior*) and 2 (*Did not project his own faults onto others*) of equal importance? Using the language test, we see that the first two words of both topics (*did not*) are the same—a good sign. Next we see that *rationalize* and *project* are both verbs—another good sign. Also we might notice that *rationalize* and *project* are psychological terms—another good sign. Eventually—after giving the matter careful thought—we will probably decide that the topics are coordinate. Putting the rest of the outline to the same test, we would in all likelihood conclude that it is coordinate.

Testing your outline for coordination requires not only intelligence but also an appreciation of the importance of this step in writing. A lopsided outline, though perhaps better than none at all, is of no great help to the writer. But a carefully planned outline that is logically coordinate is usually the blueprint for a superior theme.

Returning now to our original problem, that of constructing a detailed topic outline on the subject "My Best High School Teacher," we suggest that you note these important differences between the scratch outline (p. 12) and the following topic outline: (1) we do not use every item on the list; (2) the main divisions (I and II) and the subtopics under the first main division (A and B) are not to be found on the scratch outline; (3) we use a minimum number of main divisions as a way of limiting our subject, *saying more and more about less and less.*

MY BEST TEACHER

Introduction
I. At school
   A. Outstanding as teacher
      1. Treated all students fairly
      2. Gave students personal assistance
      3. Knew his subject thoroughly
      4. Spent minimum time lecturing
      5. Kept students busy with drills and themes
      6. Used films and recordings
   B. Successful as coach and sponsor
      1. Coached baseball team
      2. Sponsored yearbook
II. Away from school
   A. Directed community theater
   B. Pitched for semipro baseball team
Conclusion

A frequent criticism of student writing is that it is vague. The writer does not give sufficient examples and illustrations to explain his general ideas. An easy way to avoid this criticism is to use the three-level outline even for short themes. By a three-level outline we do not mean an outline with three main divisions. The following outline entitled "A Major Decision" has two main divisions, but it is a three-level outline. I and II are the first level; A and B under I and A and B under II are the second level; and the 1 and 2 under the several subtopics make the third level. Note that in the first main division we have 1 and 2 under A but do not have 1 and 2 under B. This arrangement is acceptable. The general rule in outlining is that anything you divide should be separated into two or more parts. Obviously if you are dividing an apple you cannot split it into fewer than two parts; otherwise, you will not be dividing it. The same principle holds for outlining.

A MAJOR DECISION

Introduction
I. Staying in the Army
   A. Advantages
      1. Early retirement
      2. Opportunity for travel
   B. Disadvantages
II. Becoming a civilian
   A. Advantages
      1. Greater freedom
      2. Chance to be part of community
   B. Disadvantages
      1. Lack of security
      2. Limited opportunity to travel
Conclusion

Using a three-level outline even for a short theme is highly recommended, for in moving to the third level you will be giving concrete examples and illustrations, thus helping to avoid vagueness in your theme.

Using 3″ × 5″ Index Cards

Discovering and organizing the main divisions is a major problem for some students. Thus, the basic weakness of a theme can often be traced to faulty generalizations, especially in forming the broad categories. Students usually agree that once they have outlined their main divisions the subtopics fall into place. But suppose you have trouble in deciding upon your main divisions. Are there any practical ways to solve this problem?

One solution is to use 3″ × 5″ index cards or small slips of paper. Write your thoughts as they come to your mind. Put only one idea or thought on a card. As you jot down your ideas do not worry about spelling, punctuation, or grammar. Concentrate on content; you will be more relaxed and your thoughts should flow freely. After you have jotted down as many ideas and facts as you can think of concerning the topic of your theme, stop for a minute and try to think of two or more divisions into which you can separate the cards. Perhaps your reasons may not be perfectly clear to you at the beginning, but even if you have only a vague notion of how to state the main divisions in your outline, you can still go ahead and separate the cards into groups that seem to have a common quality. Often this common quality will become clearer to you as you arrange the cards, and by the time you have finished you will know the precise reason for your divisions. You may find that some of the cards do not fit into any of the groups; these are probably *deadwood* and should be discarded.

As we have suggested, after you have divided the cards, ask yourself for each group, "Why did I put these cards into this group?" When you answer this question you will have one main division. In like manner you will determine your other main divisions. After you have listed these divisions on a sheet of paper, study them to make sure they are in proper order. If you are writing a theme on "Admirable Traits" and have discovered three main divisions (*honesty, humor, ambition*), be sure to have a definite reason for the order in which you arrange them.

For instance, if *honesty* were considered the most important trait, it might be listed first. *Humor*, then, could come in the middle as being the least important. And *ambition* would come last because the writer is going to devote more space to discussing this trait, placing it at the end so it will make a stronger impression on the reader. If you were writing a theme using the same main divisions, you might want to order them differently, which would be perfectly all right as long as you had some intelligent reason for the arrangement. As you can see, a logical organizational pattern communicates important ideas to the sensitive reader as clearly as the ideas that are actually stated in the sentences.

After you have your main divisions in proper order, go over the cards once more, putting the ideas and facts in logical order under the main divisions already listed on your topic outline. Again you may want to discard some ideas or facts and add others, keeping in mind the length of your theme. But the important thing is that you have constructed a helpful plan. Your theme will be easier to write, for you have a better idea of what you want to say.

Parallel Topics

After you have done your best to make your outline *coordinate*, you are ready to tackle the final phase in perfecting it, expressing the topics in language that is parallel in form. Perhaps the best way to understand this technique is to see how it applies to a specific outline.

TEEN-AGE NARCOTICS ADDICTION

Introduction
  I. Causes
    A. Poor housing conditions
    B. Improper supervision of children by parents
    C. Inadequate enforcement of narcotics laws
  II. Effects
    A. School dropouts
    B. Increase in crime
      1. Burglaries
      2. Shoplifting
    C. Malnutrition
  III. Remedies
    A. Government clinics in big cities
      1. Medical treatment
      2. Psychological counseling
    B. Special vocational schools
    C. Agency to find suitable jobs
Conclusion

At the outset, it might help you to know that the outline is parallel. Also we might add that in making an outline it is wise to use noun constructions—if at all possible—because nouns usually say something definite. Your outline will be more effective if it is specific rather than general. Now let us examine the outline carefully to see why it is parallel. First, let us look at the main divisions: *Causes, Effects,* and *Remedies.* If we place these words side by side, we can see that they are similar in form, even though we do not know the parts of speech. You do not have to be an expert in grammar to make a logical outline, but you do have to use your common sense and your innate sense of balance and proportion. However, to be specific, the three main divisions are nouns, parallel in form.

How about the A, B, and C under I? Here it is a little more difficult to see the parallel pattern, because the modifiers are different from one another. But in striving for parallelism in your outline you should not worry about the modifiers; if the key words in the related topics are in the same form, the topics are parallel. In this case the key words are parallel: (A) *conditions,* (B) *enforcement,* and (C) *supervision.*

The same thing is true in the second main division, *Effects*—(A) *dropouts,* (B) *increase,* and (C) *malnutrition,* the key words, are parallel nouns. How about 1 and 2 under IIB? Without even knowing the parts of speech, your common sense should tell you that they are parallel, because both are specific types of crime and both are obviously in the same language form.

In the third main division, *Remedies,* the key words of A, B, and C (*clinics, schools,* and *agency*) are parallel nouns. Although they are modified differently, the key words are in the same form, which is all that is needed for parallel structure. Moreover, subtopics 1 and 2 under IIIA are parallel with each other, because the key words (*treatment* and *counseling*) are both nouns. Thus we see that the overall outline is parallel.

Now let us consider an outline that is not parallel.

PROGRESS IN TREATING MENTAL ILLS

Introduction
  I. What was the situation a century ago?
     A. The conditions in the asylums were deplorable.
     B. Public attitude
     C. Having little concern for patients
 II. Situation today
     A. The attitude of the public is changing.
     B. Modern advances
        1. Using shock therapy
        2. To use tranquilizers
III. What does the future hold?
     A. The general public will probably look upon mental illness as no different from physical ailments.
     B. Advances in therapy
Conclusion

Before comparing the topics, we wish to make two statements about outlining in general. First, questions should not be used in outlines, for invariably they are not as clear as declarative statements. Questions can be effective in stimulating the reader, but the outline is meant to help you—not to impress the reader. Second, complete sentences should not be used in a topic outline nor should punctuation appear at the end of the topics.

Now we are ready to examine the main divisions of the sample outline. Note that the first and third main divisions violate the principle that we have just mentioned. Then, in order to make the main divisions parallel with each other, we have to change the questions to topics similar in form to the second main division.

    I. Situation a century ago
   II. Situation today
  III. Hopes for future progress

Realizing that A, B, and C under the first main division should be parallel with each other (but not necessarily with I, II, and III) we must find some way to get rid of the complete sentence in topic A. We find a key word, *conditions*, and then change the sentence to a phrase that is parallel with B.

    A. Conditions in asylums
    B. Public attitude

Further, we notice that C is different from A and B, so we also change C to a noun phrase.

    A. Conditions in asylums
    B. Public attitude
    C. Treatment of patients

We move on to the second main division and apply the same test, changing the complete sentence to a topic comparable to B.

    A. Public attitude
    B. Modern advances

Then we see that 1 and 2 under B should be changed to make them parallel with each other (but not necessarily with A and B), for *using* is a gerund and *to use* is an infinitive. We decide to change them in this manner.

    1. Use of shock treatment
    2. Use of tranquilizers

The subtopics of the third main division also must be revised. We have already changed III to a topic; but A and B are not parallel, because A is a complete sentence. So we convert the sentence to a topic that is similar to B and come up with this parallel pattern:

    A. Public attitude
    B. Advances in therapy

Having made the necessary changes, we are now ready to rewrite our out-

line with the assurance that it is parallel as well as coordinate and that it is a clear blueprint for writing an intelligent theme.

PROGRESS IN TREATING MENTAL ILLS

Introduction
  I. Situation a century ago
     A. Conditions in asylums
     B. Public attitude
     C. Treatment of patients
 II. Situation today
     A. Public attitude
     B. Modern advances
        1. Use of shock therapy
        2. Use of tranquilizers
III. Hopes for future progress
     A. Public attitude
     B. Advances in therapy
Conclusion

Although we have separated the two principles *coordination* and *parallelism* for the sake of a clearer explanation, you have probably noticed that they are very closely linked. After you have had some experience in outlining, you will probably develop the knack of making your outline coordinate and parallel at the same time, eliminating the last step we have described. Obviously if your outline is coordinate it has a better chance of being parallel, and if it is parallel it has a better chance of being coordinate. But the important thing is that your outline be positive, a clear blueprint of the ideas you want to convey to the reader, so you will know what you want to say before you start writing your theme. Once you have grasped the technique of outlining, you will not only write a better theme but also save time in false starts and time-consuming revisions. As you move along in college and begin to take more advanced courses in which term papers are required, the ability to use an outline effectively will often be the difference between failure and success.

EXERCISE 1

Arrange the following items in a two-level topic outline. The following suggestions may be helpful:

1. A two-level outline may have more than two main divisions.
2. An outline is usually easier to construct if the main divisions are first
   listed in logical order.
3. The main divisions should be coordinate—that is, equal in value or
   importance with each other.

TELEVISION AND BEHAVIOR

Introduction
Encourages families to spend more time together
Hinders development of true sense of identity
Noncommercial educational channels sponsored by government
Beneficial effects
More extensive use of the closed circuit TV in classrooms
Future possibilities
Keeps people from getting needed exercise
Teaches false sense of values
Provides basic scientific knowledge
Keeps people posted on current events
Harmful effects
Conclusion

_____

_____

_____

_____

_____

_____

_____

_____

_____

_____

_____

_____

_____

_____

_____

_____

_____

_____

_____

_____

_____

EXERCISE 2

Rework the following outline to make it parallel. (The present chronological *(time)* arrangement should not be changed.) The following suggestions may be helpful:

1. Complete sentences or questions should not be used in a topic outline.
2. Main divisions should be parallel with each other—but not necessarily parallel with their subtopics.
3. The A, B, and C (the second level) should be parallel with each other—but not necessarily parallel with the 1 and 2 (third level).

THE SENIOR TRIP

Introduction
I. We boarded the train at one o'clock on Sunday afternoon.
   A. Spent several hours observing the countryside
   B. Playing cards and chatting
   C. We took catnaps after the lights on the train were turned down.
II. Activities in New York
   A. We arrived on Monday morning.
      1. Boat trip around Manhattan
      2. We spent the evening at Radio City Music Hall.
   B. Tuesday
      1. Made a tour of United Nations building
      2. Stroll through Central Park
      3. Visiting Museum of Modern Art
      4. We had our farewell dinner at Longchamps.
Conclusion

I. The Train
   A. Spent
   B. Played
   C. took
II.

EXERCISE 3

Arrange the following items in a three-level topic outline form. The following suggestions may be helpful:

1. The number of main divisions and the levels of subordination in an outline may be the same in number or they may be different.
2. An outline is usually easier to construct if the main divisions are first listed in logical order.
3. The main divisions should be coordinate—that is, equal with each other in value or importance.

JUVENILE DELINQUENCY

Introduction
Burglaries
Employment of both parents
Competitive sports apart from playground activities for teen-agers
Causes
Municipal agency to help teen-agers find full-time and part-time jobs
Lack of trade and vocational schools
Traffic violations
Separation of parents
Housing projects away from business districts
Effects
Vandalism
Sex crimes
School life
Misdemeanors
Lack of counseling and aptitude testing
Home life
Felonies
Remedies
Conclusion

_____

_____

_____

_____

_____

_____

EXERCISE 4

Rework the following outline to make it parallel. (The present order of the main divisions and subtopics should not be changed.) The following suggestions may be helpful:

1. Complete sentences or questions should not be used in a topic outline.
2. Main divisions should be parallel with each other—but not necessarily parallel with their subtopics.
3. The A, B, and C (second level) should be parallel with each other—but not necessarily parallel with the 1 and 2 (third level).

AUTOMATION—BLESSING OR CURSE?

Introduction
  I. What are the immediate benefits?
     A. Automation usually provides improved health and safety conditions.
     B. Higher wages and more leisure for skilled workers
 II. Immediate dangers
     A. More unskilled workers are put out of jobs.
     B. Increase mortality of small business
     C. There is a danger of a serious depression because of the overproduction of consumer goods.
III. One must consider certain unpredictable factors.
     A. Effect on foreign trade
     B. If the number of unemployed becomes much greater Communist groups in this country may exploit the situation and gain a foothold.
     C. Overemphasis on technical education
Conclusion

_____

_____

_____

_____

_____

_____

_____

_____

_____

_____

EXERCISE 5

Arrange the following items in a three-level topic outline form. The following suggestions may be helpful:

1. The number of main divisions and the levels of subordination in an outline may be the same in number or they may be different.
2. An outline is usually easier to construct if the main divisions are first listed in logical order.
3. The main divisions should be coordinate—that is, equal in value or importance with each other.

THINK BEFORE YOU WRITE

Introduction
Three or four-level outline to assure sufficient facts and examples
No stress on mechanics
Organizing the theme
Writing legibly and neatly
Elimination of ideas or facts that do not logically fit into groups
Eliminating deadwood
Ideas on $3'' \times 5''$ cards as they come to your mind
Main divisions of outline stated or suggested in introduction
Paying close attention to spelling, punctuation, sentence structure, etc.
Thought cards into groups or divisions
Writing the theme
Final draft
First draft
Divisions put in logical order
No fancy or ornate language
Conclusion

_____

_____

_____

_____

_____

_____

_____

_____

EXERCISE 6

Rework the following outline to make it parallel. (The present order of the main divisions and subtopics should not be changed.) The following suggestions may be helpful:

1. Complete sentences or questions should not be used in a topic outline.
2. Main divisions should be parallel with each other—but not necessarily parallel with their subtopics.
3. The A, B, and C (second level) should be parallel with each other but not necessarily with the 1 and 2 (third level).

GRADING THE STUDENT

Introduction

I. The grouping of students varies according to the size and policy of the school.
  A. Heterogeneous method one way of grouping students
    1. This type of grouping includes students of varied abilities.
    2. Wide distribution of scores and letter grades
  B. Homogeneous
    1. Students of comparable abilities grouped together
    2. Narrow distribution of grades
II. Measuring
  A. The teacher can observe pupils directly over an extended period.
  B. Essay and objective tests
  C. Conduct and attitude additional factors
III. Appraising as distinguished from measuring
  A. Using the standard curve for letter grades
  B. Some teachers grade the student according to his achievement in relation to his ability.
  C. Sometimes the teacher grades the student according to an objective standard apart from classroom work.
    1. Civil Service tests are sometimes used as a basis.
    2. College entrance exams

Conclusion

_____

_____

_____

_____

_____

Lesson 2

Introduction and Conclusion

The Introduction

Perhaps the most important part of your paper is the introduction. The reader passes judgment on an article or essay after reading the first paragraph and often—unless obliged for professional reasons to read it to the end—will move on to an article that has greater appeal. Thus, the conscientious writer will want to make his introduction effective by using a few basic techniques and by avoiding certain pitfalls.

Appropriate title

A well chosen title can be an important adjunct to your introduction; in fact, it is a kind of miniature introduction. Since the title should suggest the subject of your paper, choose it with care, striving for one that is clear, pointed, and brief. However, scrupulously avoid the assumption that your title is *per se* part of your introduction. Such an assumption leads to the following unacceptable practice.

Title	A PASSION FOR THE UGLY
Poor	This seems to be a common problem with many people in today's society if our city streets and highways can be used as an example.
Better	A close look at the majority of homes and commercial buildings in our cities and towns would suggest that our American forebears had (to borrow a phrase from H. L. Mencken) a "libido for the ugly."
Comments	In the first example the writer apparently tries to save time by letting *this* refer in a general way to the title instead of making a precise reference. Such a practice is to be avoided.
Title	OUR SENIOR TRIP TO NEW YORK
Poor	This was one of the most enjoyable trips I ever took in my life, although I was exhausted by the time I got back home.
Better	When the special train, crowded with sixty screaming teen-agers, inched out of Union Station in Evansville for New York City, the conductor probably wished that he had taken a nice quiet job in a boiler factory.
Comments	The writer of the poor introduction makes the same mistake as does the writer of the poor introduction in the first example, namely, assuming that the title is inherently part of the introduction. Note how the second writer avoids this problem.

Poor Introductions

When receiving instructions we usually expect to be told what to do and how to do it (how many eggs to put into the cake mix or how to hold the tennis racket while serving), and you may wonder why this chapter accentuates the negative. It does so in the beginning because a list of rules about what to do might cramp your style. The introduction to your theme can reflect your originality—your personality—and too many directions can inhibit your expression. Yet a few minutes spent studying these examples of poor beginnings will help you guard against some all-too-common mistakes. Here are a few introductions that make the average reader groan and stop reading.

Do not call the reader's attention to the fact that you are writing a theme.

Title	GOING STEADY
Poor	In this theme I am going to discuss the advantages and disadvantages of teen-agers going steady.
Better	Although going steady solves certain problems for the teen-age boy and girl, such as a date for Saturday night, this practice leads to conflicts that can be detrimental to the normal development of the individual.
Title	CHEATING IN COLLEGE
Poor	The purpose of my theme is to convince the reader that cheating in college has a bad effect on the person who does this type of thing.
Better	The student who cheats or plagiarizes in college is actually cheating himself, for one's personal happiness depends largely on knowing and accepting his limitations as well as his strong points.

Do not apologize! The composition teacher generally does not expect you to be an authority on the topic about which you are writing.

Title	THE FIREARMS ISSUE
Poor	Although I haven't had a chance to read very much about this topic, I feel that guns and ammunition should not be sold to persons unless they have a permit that proves they are responsible citizens.
Better	The tragic assassination of President Kennedy brought to sharp focus in the minds of many thoughtful citizens a question that has for too many years been brushed aside. Should firearms be sold indiscriminately on the open market to anyone who wants to buy them?

Do not complain about your lack of interest in the topic.

Title	"NO MAN IS AN ISLAND"
Poor	I really don't have very much interest in British literature, so my interpretation of John Donne's prose poem may not be exactly what you want. However, I do enjoy reading the short stories of Edgar Allan Poe, and I feel that I could do a much better job explaining the symbolism in "The Fall of the House of Usher."
Better	Although the relationship between John Donne's "No Man Is an Island" and Edgar Allan Poe's "The Fall of the House of Usher" is not readily apparent, both literary works suggest basic concepts in modern psychology that convince me that the authors were profound thinkers far ahead of their times.

Title	STEREOTYPED THINKING
Poor	The essay by Walter Lippmann dealing with this topic was very hard to understand. I'm sure I could write a better theme on something I am more interested in. Nevertheless I will try my best.
Better	If one thinks seriously about how he thinks—approaching the matter honestly—he will probably agree with the observation of Walter Lippmann in his penetrating book *Public Opinion* that much of our thinking is based on preconceived ideas that have been acquired through environmental influences rather than from objective truth. The person who realizes this is in a better position to cope with problems and get along with people who hold dissimilar views.

Effective Introductions

Now that we have suggested several things not to do, we can concentrate on the positive aspect of writing a good introduction. How long should it be? The length of the introduction depends largely on the length of your paper, a short theme of two or three pages requiring a paragraph of two or three sentences (or possibly one long sentence). A longer composition—say a reference paper of ten or fifteen pages—may require a whole page for a clear exposition of the central idea. Your sense of proportion should guide you in this matter; no exact formula can be given. Remember that the introduction and conclusion are *not* main divisions of your theme. (This is the reason we did not place Roman numerals before the words *Introduction* and *Conclusion* in the sample outlines in Chapter 1.) Using Roman numerals might lead to an outline like this one:

I. Introduction
II. Going steady
III. Conclusion

From the above outline we would have to conclude that the writer had not divided his theme into at least two main parts, thus violating a cardinal principle in outlining and running the risk of writing a lopsided theme. Therefore, it is preferable to write only the words *Introduction* and *Conclusion* at the beginning and end of your outline to remind you that your theme (short or long) should have these components.

Unless told otherwise, you will ordinarily not be expected to use a rhetorical device (such as a question, exclamation, or direct quotation) as part of your introduction, although some writers frequently do use such an opening to arrest the reader's attention. *The important thing is to state briefly and clearly the main idea of your composition in language that is natural and direct.* In other words, give the reader a *general* idea of what your theme is going to be about in *general* terms, saving the concrete details and specific examples for the main parts of your paper.

Usually a hard look at the title and the main divisions of the outline (assuming that the title is precise and the outline is logical) will help you to write an effective introduction. But this technique will not work unless you have limited your topic by converting it into a subject. The initial topic of a theme or report is often a broad generality, but the subject should be a limited aspect of the broader idea. For example, the topic of your theme might be the *Civil War*, but you may finally decide to write on the surrender of General Lee at Appomattox. The next time you have to write a theme, try to recall this rule of thumb: *Say more and more about less and less.* Notice how the following topics have been limited even before the main divisions of the outline have been stated.

Topic	Subject
Socialized Medicine	Hospitalization for the Elderly
Urban Renewal	The Hardships Caused by Urban Renewal
Civil Rights	The Problems of Minority Groups in Large Cities
High School Sports	Are High School Sports Overemphasized?
Teen-Age Drivers	The Alarming Accident Rate Among Teen-Age Drivers
Federal Aid to Schools	The Need for Federal Aid to Parochial Schools

Having limited the topic, you are ready to form the main divisions of the outline, then to study the title and the main divisions for help in writing a clear introduction, which will lead naturally to your first main point. For example:

THE HARDSHIPS CAUSED BY URBAN RENEWAL

Introduction
  I. Scarcity of low-rent housing
  II. Dislocation of small businesses
Conclusion

Driving or walking through the commercial district of a large American city one may be greatly impressed by the demolition of old buildings and the construction of ornate motels and soaring office buildings in their place. But consider for a moment the personal hardships that this "progress" is causing to thousands of displaced people who cannot find adequate housing and to the small businessmen who cannot afford to rebuild their condemned grocery stores and barber shops.

THE PROBLEMS OF MINORITY GROUPS IN BIG CITIES

Introduction
  I. Jobs
 II. Housing
III. Medical care
Conclusion

Although the underprivileged groups in our large cities are getting a fairer shake today than they did a decade ago, many problems—especially those related to earning a decent living—are still to be solved if all Americans are to gain the human dignity that we consider a birthright.

The *introduction*, then, is a general statement of the central idea that you intend to amplify in the main part of your paper. One of the simplest ways (and possibly the best way) to form such a generalization is to relate your title to the main divisions of your outline. Use language that will arrest the reader's attention and make him want to read your paper to the end. Composing a good introduction is an opportunity to use your imagination, so you will want to give it careful thought. Remember that an effective introduction is one of the most important features of a superior theme or report.

The Conclusion

Having written your introduction and having presented detailed information to develop your subject in the main part of your paper, you are now ready to write the conclusion. The length of your paper is an important element in your decision about what type of conclusion to use. If you are writing a reference paper of ten to twenty pages, you will usually need a summary conclusion restating the main points of your paper. But if you are writing a short theme of three or four hundred words, a summary conclusion may be awkward—worse than no conclusion at all. However, as in our discussion of the introduction, before pointing out the positive features let us look at some types that should be avoided.

Poor Conclusions

In writing a short theme do not mechanically sum up the main points of your discourse.

ADMIRABLE TRAITS

Introduction
I. Honesty
II. Ambition
III. Humor
Conclusion

Poor   In conclusion, the traits I find most admirable in the other person are honesty, ambition, and humor.

Better   I sincerely believe that a person who is basically honest and who has great determination—moderated, of course, by a warm sense of humor—will gain not only worldly success but also much personal happiness.

MY FAVORITE OUTDOOR SPORTS

Introduction
I. Swimming
II. Hunting
III. Fishing
Conclusion

Poor   My favorite outdoor sports, therefore, are swimming, hunting, and fishing.

Better   Although sometimes my friends accuse me of being a hermit, there is nothing more relaxing to me (when the demands of civilization begin to ring in my ears) than a solitary swim in a cool lake or a trek through the woods on a brisk autumn day or a boat drift down the river with fishing as an excuse. Without the outdoor sports I love, life would be dull indeed.

Do not belabor the fact that you are writing a conclusion.

GOING STEADY

Introduction
I. Advantages
II. Disadvantages
Conclusion

Poor   In conclusion I would like to say that going steady while still in high school has certain advantages and disadvantages.

Better   Benjamin Franklin in his autobiography said that the great benefit of being reasonable is it helps you to find a good reason for anything you have a mind to do. Thus, most of us—whether we are going steady or playing the field—will have a tendency to justify our position by giving the "good" reasons for our behavior and to overlook the "real" reasons. Now and then it might be wise to view our situations more objectively, for the attitudes we form in our youth will greatly affect our future happiness.

CHEATING IN COLLEGE

Introduction
I. Run risk of getting expelled
II. Endanger personal development
Conclusion

Poor	After considering the pros and cons of the subject I have come to the conclusion that a person shouldn't cheat in college because such a practice may lead to psychological problems in later life.
Better	Thus, the person who cheats in college is really cheating himself. For most of the profound moral thinkers of all ages (from Socrates to Erich Fromm) agree on this fundamental truth: Man's happiness depends to a large extent on self-knowledge, especially in understanding and accepting our limitations. Therefore, the student who cheats in college is not only deluding himself but is also forming habits that could be disastrous.

Do not apologize for your lack of interest in or knowledge of the subject on which you are writing.

NO MAN IS AN ISLAND

Introduction

  I. "Meditation 17" by John Donne

 II. *For Whom the Bell Tolls* by Ernest Hemingway

Conclusion

Poor	Although, as I said in the introduction, I have no great interest in British literature, I probably could have done a better job in writing this theme if I had had more time to read something about the life of John Donne.
Better	Thus, one does not have to have a background in British literature to appreciate the beauty and profundity of this famous prose poem by John Donne. For the theme that he so clearly articulates is the great problem in our contemporary world: the necessity of a true brotherhood of man under the Fatherhood of God. "Therefore, never send to know for whom the bell tolls. It tolls for thee."

STEREOTYPED THINKING

Introduction

  I. Childhood environment

 II. Books read and movies seen

Conclusion

Poor	As I stated at the beginning of this theme I am not absolutely certain I understand what Walter Lippmann means by stereotyped thinking, although this is my fault and not the fault of the author.
Better	Realizing that many of our strong convictions result from environmental influences (most people are Republicans or Democrats because their parents were), we should as students in college make a special effort to understand both sides of controversial issues; for it is only in this way that we can develop the unprejudiced objectivity that is the hallmark of an educated man.

Effective Conclusions

So much for what *not* to do! Now let us concentrate on the positive features of writing a good conclusion. First, remember that the conclusion is important because it will impress the reader and may win him to your point of view. The final statement should be emphatic and clearly related to the central idea suggested by the introduction. The superior conclusion usually goes a step beyond what has already been said in the main body of the theme by expressing a judgment or an opinion that logically follows from the ideas developed in the composition.

The two examples that follow are worthy of imitation because they embody the qualities that should be present in an effective conclusion: (1) they are clearly related to the title and the main divisions of the outline; (2) they are emphatic; and (3) they express a judgment that goes beyond the theme itself. In other words, the writer has come to a definite conclusion instead of ending his theme abruptly as if he had run out of time or paper.

PASSION FOR THE UGLY

Introduction
 I. Homes
 II. Commercial buildings
Conclusion

There can be little doubt from the hideous architecture that surrounds us that our American forebears had a "libido for the ugly." We can only hope that this disease is not congenital and that it can be mitigated by education and other factors. But, from the grubby houses and commercial buildings still being constructed and the rubbish and junk yards that mar the beauty of our streets and highways, it seems that a passion for the ugly is still one of the basic drives of modern man.

THE FIREARMS ISSUE

Introduction
 I. Requiring permits for new weapons
 II. Registering ownership of old guns
Conclusion

It is hard to predict with certainty that a Federal law regulating the sale and possession of firearms will curtail crime and violence in the United States, but the procrastination of the U.S. Congress in this matter makes one wonder if perhaps the Senators and Representatives in Washington are involved in a conspiracy with the kingpins of the underworld to turn the cities and towns of America into asphalt jungles.

Perhaps the salty aphorism of Winston Churchill will help you to remember the necessity of making your introduction, the main divisions, and the conclusion distinct parts of your theme or report: "When writing an essay or giving a speech," said Sir Winston, "tell them what you are going to tell them. Then tell them. And then tell them that you have told them." An appealing introduction and an emphatic conclusion, then, are important parts of a successful paper, and the little extra time you spend in making these components clear and distinct may account for the difference between a poor, average, or superior theme.

EXERCISE 7

Write a short introduction and conclusion for a theme based on the titles and main divisions listed below:

INTERCOLLEGIATE ATHLETICS

Introduction
  I. Advantages
 II. Disadvantages
Conclusion

Introduction _____

_____

_____

_____

_____

_____

Conclusion _____

_____

_____

_____

_____

_____

CONFORMITY IN COLLEGE

Introduction
  I. Good aspects
 II. Bad aspects
Conclusion

Introduction _____

_____

_____

_____

_____

_____

Conclusion _____

_____

_____

_____

_____

_____

EXERCISE 8

Write a short introduction and conclusion for a theme based on the titles and main divisions listed below:

CHANGING FASHIONS IN CLOTHES

Introduction
  I. Men's
 II. Women's
Conclusion

Introduction _____

_____

_____

_____

_____

Conclusion _____

_____

_____

_____

_____

THE ENDS OF EDUCATION

Introduction
  I. Professional
 II. Cultural
Conclusion

Introduction _____

_____

_____

_____

Conclusion

Lesson 3

The Paragraph

Paragraphing can be looked upon as a form of punctuation. Just as the period at the end of a sentence indicates a complete thought, the properly constructed paragraph signals to the reader a unit of one or more sentences related to a single aspect of the central idea. Paragraphing if studied in all its ramifications can present complexities that may confuse rather than help the inexperienced writer. So we shall try to simplify the process by showing you how to use the outline as a guide or blueprint for dividing your theme into thought units that will help the reader follow your chain of ideas to a logical conclusion.

The easiest way to divide your thought units is to plan the paragraphs before you begin the actual writing of the theme, assuming, of course, that you have constructed a logical outline. Obviously the length of the theme is an important factor in planning the paragraphs. For instance, if you were writing a two-page theme (three hundred or four hundred words) from the following outline, how many paragraphs would you have?

ADMIRABLE TRAITS

Introduction
  I. Honesty

A. With himself
B. With others
II. Humor
A. Able to laugh at himself
B. Considerate of others
III. Ambition
A. In his social life
B. In his job
Conclusion

You would probably have five paragraphs: a short one for the introduction and the conclusion and three longer ones for the three main divisions. However, if you were writing a longer theme (five hundred to seven hundred words) you would no doubt have more paragraphs, for excessively long ones are often disconcerting to the reader. You would still have a paragraph for both your introduction and conclusion, but you would probably have two for each main division (one for each subtopic) or a total of eight rather than five paragraphs, enabling the reader to follow your chain of thought from central idea to conclusion.

Using your outline as a guide will help you divide your ideas into units that reflect the organizational pattern of your theme as well as test your paragraphs for unity, completeness, emphasis, and coherence before you begin the actual writing of your paper.

Unity

We mentioned *unity* in our discussion of outlining, saying that every topic and subtopic in the outline must be logically related to a central idea. No material should be introduced that digresses from the clear development of the central idea. An examination of the theme titles and the main divisions of the following outlines should reveal their unity.

MY FAVORITE OUTDOOR SPORTS	A MAJOR DECISION
Introduction	Introduction
I. Swimming	I. Staying in the Army
II. Hunting	II. Becoming a civilian
III. Fishing	Conclusion
Conclusion	

The unity principle in paragraphing is the same as that in outlining. Just as the main divisions in an outline must be directly related to the central idea of the theme, the general ideas and facts in a paragraph must be logically related to the part or parts of the theme that make up the whole. If you throw into the paragraph ideas or facts that are not logically related to the topic, you have violated the unity principle. It is much easier for most students to write a unified paragraph after studying the general ideas in an outline than to spend valuable time composing complete sentences and later making time-consuming revisions. Carefully consider the following topic outlines as examples of this principle.

GOING STEADY

Introduction
  I. Advantages
    A. Being sure of a date
    B. Not having to strain to impress your date
    C. Gaining status among fellow students
  II. Disadvantages
    A. Being bored with the same person
    B. Missing the fun of meeting new people
    C. Gaining a valuable concept of married life
    D. Becoming involved in promiscuous activity
Conclusion

Notice that IIC is out of place. *Gaining a valuable concept of married life* is more of an advantage than a disadvantage to the thoughtful teen-ager who in a few years—or sooner—may make definite marriage plans. This topic belongs under the first main division.

Students who write before they think frequently make this mistake: including an idea in one paragraph that belongs in another or inserting material that is irrelevant to the theme entirely. Consider the logical unity of the next outline.

MY BEST TEACHER

Introduction
  I. At school
    A. Effectively uses audio-visual aids
    B. Born in England
    C. Knows his subject and is good lecturer
    D. Directs senior play
  II. Away from school
    A. Pitches for semipro baseball team
    B. Directs community theater
    C. Graduated from Cambridge
    D. Ran for city council
Conclusion

In this outline are two facts (one under each main division) that are not logically related to the main topics. If you included these facts in your composition you would be violating the important principle of paragraph unity, which holds that every idea and fact in the paragraph should contribute to the development of a single topic, no matter how interesting or important the digression might be. The two facts, of course, are *born in England* and *graduated from Cambridge*.

Emphasis

In writing your theme you should not only make a serious attempt to delete irrelevant material from your paragraph but also arrange the general ideas and facts in an orderly way. In both outlining and paragraphing the proper arrangement of ideas and facts is known as *emphasis*.

Emphasis in outlining and paragraphing, then, means the conscious ordering or placement of ideas and facts to give special attention or stress to what is most important. A speaker may pound his fist on the rostrum to emphasize an important point in his address. A copywriter may underline a word in an advertisement to emphasize its importance. A girl may wear a tight dress to emphasize her figure. Similarly, the writer of a theme should arrange his ideas and facts to stress those of greater importance and de-emphasize those of lesser importance, keeping in mind his central idea and purpose.

Logical Patterns of Organization

The easiest and perhaps the best way to achieve proper paragraph emphasis is to solve this problem in your outline before you write your paragraphs. First, find an organizational plan that will emphasize what is most important in your theme. Second, arrange your main divisions in some logical order. Third, arrange your subtopics under the main divisions to indicate the relative importance of the ideas and facts.

The topic outlines that follow show definite organizational principles that give unity as well as emphasis to the paragraphs. Notice, particularly, the organizational plan for "My Favorite Sports." Often, as in this case, it makes little or no difference which main division or subtopic comes first. Here you need not worry about emphasis in arrangement, but you will want to compose a strong topic sentence to gain paragraph emphasis of another sort.

Chronological
(According to time)

OUR SENIOR TRIP

Introduction
I. Monday
II. Tuesday
III. Wednesday
Conclusion

Advantages and Disadvantages

GOING STEADY

Introduction
I. Advantages
II. Disadvantages
Conclusion

Cause and Effect

PASSION FOR THE UGLY

Introduction
I. Lack of education and
values of immigrants
II. Building of ugly homes
and buildings
Conclusion

No special difference

MY FAVORITE SPORTS

Introduction
I. Swimming
II. Hunting
III. Fishing
Conclusion

Most Important to Least Important	*Least Important to Most Important*
MY FAVORITE TEACHER	ADMIRABLE TRAITS
Introduction	Introduction
I. At school	I. Humor
II. Away from school	II. Ambition
Conclusion	III. Honesty
	Conclusion

East to West	*Small to Big*
THE BIRTH OF A NATION	URBAN RENEWAL
Introduction	Introduction
I. Settling the east coast	I. Towns
II. Development of the Midwest	II. Cities
III. Mass exodus to the West	Conclusion
Conclusion	

Up to Down	*Here to There*
OUR NEW HOME	MY TRIP TO EUROPE
Introduction	Introduction
I. First floor	I. Flew to New York
II. Second floor	II. Boarded *Queen Mary*
Conclusion	Conclusion

When we speak of *emphasis,* then, we mean a conscious ordering of ideas and facts in the topic outline and within the paragraph. In striving for *unity* (as pointed out in the preceding section) the writer tries to eliminate everything in the paragraph that is not logically related to the topic being developed. In using emphasis, on the other hand, the writer arranges his ideas and facts so that his message will be clear. The following outlines in which some of the subtopics are not in proper sequence may help you to understand and use this principle.

OUR SENIOR TRIP

Introduction
  I. Monday
    A. Arrived at Grand Central Station
    B. Ate supper at automat
    C. Spent afternoon at U.N.
    D. Spent evening at Radio City Musical Hall
  II. Tuesday
    A. Had breakfast in Central Park
    B. Went atop Empire State Building to see city by night
    C. Spent afternoon touring Wall Street area
  III. Wednesday
    A. Attended morning Mass at St. Patrick's Cathedral
    B. Caught train for Evansville around noon
Conclusion

In the first main division, you can see that subtopic B, *Ate supper at auto-mat*, is out of sequence. If the writer intended to use the chronological pattern of emphasis, he should have placed *Ate supper at automat* after *Spent afternoon at U.N.* In the second main division, subtopic B, *Went atop Empire State Building to see city by night*, should follow subtopic C, *Spent afternoon touring Wall Street area*, because of its logical order in time. The subtopics in the third main division are properly placed with respect to emphasis.

The emphasis problem in the next outline is similar to the one we have just discussed.

URBAN RENEWAL

Introduction
  I. Towns
     A. Tearing down slums
     B. Condemning slums
     C. Constructing modern homes and buildings
  II. Cities
     A. Tearing down slums
     B. Passing needed legislation
     C. Constructing modern homes and buildings
Conclusion

Careful consideration of the first main division, *Towns,* will force us to conclude that *Condemning slums* should logically come before *Tearing down slums,* for the obvious reason that the slums must be condemned before they can be torn down. Similarly, in the second main division, *Cities,* appropriate laws must first be enacted before the destruction of the slums can begin. Thus *Passing needed legislation* should come before *Tearing down slums* for proper emphasis in the outline and, especially, in the written paragraph of the theme.

The rules of paragraph unity and emphasis may seem obvious, nothing more than the application of common sense. Yet they are major problems with many writers—the experienced as well as the beginners; people write before they think and are too lazy to make the necessary revisions. Using a coordinate, parallel topic outline will improve unity and emphasis—and save considerable time.

Topic Sentence

Besides arranging your ideas and facts in a logical order, you can achieve paragraph emphasis by the proper construction and placement of the topic sentence. Again the outline is of great help, for if it is a true blueprint of what you intend to communicate, the main and subordinate ideas will stand out clearly and greatly assist you in writing a good topic sentence.

Usually the generalization or topic sentence appears at the beginning of the paragraph, but it may appear in the middle, at the end, or in more than one place, depending on the desired effect of the writer. In some instances the topic is implied rather than stated directly, but use of this technique is not recommended until you have gained proficiency in writing the standard paragraph where the topic sentence appears at the beginning or the end. Note carefully in the sample paragraphs that follow—paragraphs based on simple topic outlines—how the topics of the outline help the writer formulate a clear topic sentence that gives emphasis to the paragraph.

MY FAVORITE OUTDOOR SPORTS

Introduction
I. Swimming
    A. Excellent physical exercise
    B. Good way to meet people
    C. Reasonable cost
    D. Available facilities
II. Hunting
    A.
    B.
    C.
III. Fishing
    A.
    B.
    C.
Conclusion

Swimming, to be sure, is my favorite outdoor sport for a number of practical reasons. It is generally agreed that swimming is one of the best forms of exercise in which a person can participate, because most of the muscles of the body are brought into play—rather than just a few as in other sports. Besides, a person often has an opportunity to meet new and interesting friends—especially of the opposite sex—on the beach or at the swimming pool. (Perhaps this is the main reason I like swimming.) But there are also other less personal reasons why I prefer to swim than, say, to play golf. The initial cost in equipment and usually the admission fee are much less than in golf—not to mention the availability of facilities. In every part of the United States—depending, of course, on the time of the year—a person can easily find a swimming pool or beach facility, whereas golf courses (as well as tennis courts) are scarce or terribly overcrowded.

Analysis   The topic sentence comes at the beginning and states in capsule form the main idea of the paragraph, namely, the fact that the writer prefers swimming over other sports for a number of practical reasons. Making a definite effort to use a topic sentence will crystallize in your own mind the main point you are trying to get across. This awareness in turn will help you to give proper emphasis to the details that explain the generalization.

A MAJOR DECISION

Introduction
I. Staying in the Army
    A. Opportunity to travel

    B. Chance for formal education
    C. Early retirement
  II. Becoming a civilian
    A. Could settle in one place
    B. Easier to choose friends
    C. Can use more initiative
Conclusion

My greatest pleasure in life is travel, seeing the faraway places with the strange sounding names. Without a doubt I would have greater chance for travel as a soldier than as a civilian. Also, I would have an opportunity to further my education and eventually receive a college degree at government expense. Of no less importance, I could retire when I am forty years old—when most men are just getting settled in a lifetime job. I took all these advantages as well as the disadvantages into account before I finally decided to make a career of the Army. It was not an easy decision to make. I would not be free to settle in one place and become an active member of the community. Also, freedom to choose my friends on the basis of common interests would be curtailed as would my capacity to take initiative in matters affecting my personal life.

Analysis The topic sentence in the preceding paragraph is in the middle. "I took all these advantages as well as the disadvantages into account before I finally decided to make a career of the Army." Notice how the writer worked toward the topic sentence and then worked away from it. This is a legitimate technique, recommended to give variety to your paragraphs.

MY BEST TEACHER

Introduction
  I. At school
    A. Had a thorough knowledge of his subject
    B. Had the ability to communicate his knowledge
    C. Was firm but pleasant in the classroom
    D. Did an excellent job in directing class play
  II. Away from school
Conclusion

Mr. Chandler was one of those rare teachers who not only had a comprehensive knowledge of his subject but also had the ability to impart his knowledge to the students. To achieve this goal, he would not tolerate any horseplay during class, although he would often make a pun or tell a humorous story to relieve the tension. Besides being a gifted science teacher, he was also a talented drama coach. And in spite of his self-effacing attempt to give the students all the credit, everyone knew that the success of our senior play was mainly the result of his magic touch. The remarkable thing about Mr. Chandler was the fact that he was not only a superb teacher and a tireless sponsor of extracurricular events but also a model citizen from the standpoint of community affairs.

Analysis   All the details in the first part of the paragraph relate to Mr. Chandler's school activities. Although this fact is implied, it is not actually stated until the last sentence.

You can see from the three examples given that the topic sentence can come at the beginning, in the middle, or at the end.

You can gain paragraph emphasis, then, by writing a clear topic sentence that sums up the main idea of the paragraph so the reader will not be forced to draw his own conclusion from the bare facts. You can also gain paragraph emphasis, as previously explained, by arranging your ideas and facts so the reader will know at a glance (without backtracking and rereading) the relative importance of the details and their logical relationship to the central idea. The extra time you spend on making your outline emphatic and the thought you give to composing a strong topic sentence will improve the effectiveness of your paragraphs and, thus, the overall quality of your writing.

Coherence

An effective paragraph is not only unified and emphatic but also coherent; that is, the relationship to the preceding paragraph as well as the connection between ideas within the paragraph is clearly stated or implied. A theme or report, ideally, should be a tissue of logical relationships. In the first place, the main divisions should be arranged according to a logical plan (such as one of those previously mentioned: chronological, advantages and disadvantages, cause and effect, most important to least important, least important to most important, east to west, small to big, up to down, or here to there), which should be expressed or implied by transitional words, phrases, sentences, or paragraphs.

For example, suppose you were asked to write a theme on "Admirable Traits" and had formulated the following outline based on the *most important to least important* organizational plan.

ADMIRABLE TRAITS

Introduction
  I. Honesty
 II. Service to others
III. Humor
Conclusion

After treating the first main division, *Honesty*, you should not move abruptly to the second main division without a smooth transition. You can use several different types of bridges to span the divide.

(1) Repeat the first main idea: "Besides being honest with himself and with others, my ideal man will take an active interest in the welfare of his fellowmen."

(2) Use an arabic number: "The *second* trait that my ideal man should possess is social consciousness, a deep concern for the welfare of his fellowmen."

(3) Use a connecting adverb (such as *moreover, furthermore,* etc.): "Furthermore, if a man is to succeed in the true sense of the word, he must display a deep concern for his fellowmen."

Just as the writer should indicate the logical relationship between the main divisions of his essay, he should also use transitional devices within his paragraphs. Some writers have only two transitional words in their vocabulary: *and* and *but*. The first-rate writer, on the other hand, consistently uses transitions to indicate the precise relationship between ideas. Sometimes, though, the relationship is so apparent that a transitional word or phrase is superfluous, especially if the student has used a good topic outline as a blueprint for his theme. But most student themes suffer from a lack rather than a glut of transitional words and phrases.

Before writing your next theme, study the following list with the intention of using more transitional words and phrases to give coherence to your paragraphs and to bridge the gap between the main divisions of your theme.

I. *Coordinate conjunctions*

and
but
for
nor
or

II. *Correlative conjunctions*

not only . . . but also
neither . . . nor
either . . . or
both . . . and

III. *Subordinate conjunctions*

if
when
lest
after
while
until
since
before
unless
because
whether
although

IV. *Connecting adverbs and conjunctions requiring a semicolon between independent clauses*

so
yet
thus
then
hence
however
moreover
therefore
furthermore
consequently
nevertheless

V. *Other transitional words and phrases*

first
second
third
for example
for instance
in other words
on the other hand
of still greater importance
another point to bear in mind

Completeness

In addition to *unity* (every idea and fact relating to a single topic), *emphasis* (the ideas and facts being logically ordered), and *coherence* (the relationship between sentences being clearly implied or expressed), the paragraph should also be *complete*.

Completeness, though the last principle we shall discuss, is in certain respects the most important feature of a paragraph. It constitutes a serious problem for many student writers if teachers' commentaries on graded themes can be used as an indication: "Underdeveloped paragraph. Insufficient facts and examples to develop general ideas. Too many short and undeveloped paragraphs!"

Although some students overload their paragraphs with facts and examples, the majority err in the other direction: their paragraphs are too generalized. Thus, their writing is vague and sometimes illogical because the general ideas are not properly qualified by specific examples.

How can you be sure that your paragraphs are not overloaded or underdeveloped? One way is to use a detailed topic outline (even for shorter themes) to marshal facts and examples before you write your paragraphs. When you are writing your theme you have many problems to contend with at the same time: the meaning you are trying to convey in a particular sentence, the level of diction you should use, and the punctuation and sentence structure that are needed. As a matter of fact, you have to think of so many things that you can easily overlook an important point in effective writing—the necessity of including in your paragraphs sufficient facts and examples to clearly explain your generalizations.

You can avoid underdeveloped paragraphs by carefully organizing your facts in an outline before you start to write. It is relatively easy, while making your outline, to move to the third level (or even the fourth level for longer themes) and list facts and examples while the general ideas are fresh in your mind. The following sample outline, we hope, will clarify this technique and convince you of the value of organizing your facts before you write your paragraphs.

ADMIRABLE TRAITS

Introduction
  I. Humor
    A. Able to laugh at himself
    B. Considerate of others
      1. Never plays practical jokes
      2. Never laughs at misfortunes of others
      3. Never puts a person in embarrassing position
      4. Never ridicules others' faults
  II. Ambition
 III. Honesty
    A. With himself
      1. Seeks criticism of his writing
      2. Studies psychology to gain self-knowledge
      3. Asks students for evaluation

B. With others
 1. Does not engage in flattery
 2. Pays bills on time
 3. Does not brag
 4. Does not use people
Conclusion

If you followed this outline closely and submitted it with your theme or report, the experienced reader, who studied the outline before he read the paper, could make certain predictions about your theme—and probably be right. First, the second main division would probably be underdeveloped. Second, the paragraph for the first subtopic under *Humor* would probably be too short, while the second paragraph (IB) would probably be too long. The third main division, *Honesty*, would probably have better balance than the other two, although IIIB might also be a little too long.

To forestall these problems in paragraphing and to produce a more balanced theme the writer should rethink his outline rather than make major revisions after writing the first draft. He would have a better chance of writing effective paragraphs if he followed this revised outline:

ADMIRABLE TRAITS
Introduction
 I. Humor
  A. Able to laugh at himself
   1. Kids about his failures
   2. Kids about his bald head
  B. Considerate of others
   1. Never plays practical jokes
   2. Never laughs at misfortunes of others
   3. Never ridicules others' faults
 II. Ambition
  A. In his social life
   1. Enjoys being officer in clubs
   2. Likes to have many friends
  B. In his job
   1. Takes evening course at university
   2. Works out new teaching systems
 III. Honesty
  A. With himself
   1. Seeks criticism of his writing
   2. Studies psychology to gain self-knowledge
   3. Asks students for evaluation
  B. With others
   1. Does not engage in false flattery
   2. Does not "use" people for own ends
Conclusion

Arranging your ideas in such a way may seem mechanical and uninspiring; but unless you make such an attempt to organize your thoughts—either on paper or in your mind's eye—before you start writing your theme, you run the risk of having either overloaded or underdeveloped paragraphs. Your theme will reflect your lopsided thinking and lack the balance expected of good writing.

Remember, then, that your paragraphs will be more effective if you strive for *unity, emphasis, coherence,* and *completeness.* This is a rather large order for the inexperienced writer. But you can more readily achieve these important qualities in paragraphing if you will study your outline carefully with these ideas in mind before you begin the actual writing of your theme or report.

EXERCISE 9

Completeness is one of the important qualities of a good paragraph. All too often the paragraphs students write contain only vague ideas unsupported by examples and illustrations. An effective paragraph, on the other hand, gives sufficient facts to develop the topic so the writer's intention is unmistakenly clear to the reader. The outline that follows may be considered correct in all respects except that it is *incomplete*. You are to give additional subtopics under each main division from your own experience and reading. You might also try to develop the topics already given by adding subtopics on the third level of subordination or move to the third level [I (first level), A (second level), 1 (third level)] in adding your new topics under the main divisions.

EDUCATION NEVER ENDS

Introduction
  I. Preschool years
     A. Learning to talk by imitation
     B. Learning to get along with playmates
 II. Grade school years
     A. Learning the basic tools of knowledge
     B. Learning to respect and cooperate with teachers
III. High school years
     A. Learning to be a productive citizen
     B. Taking courses in preparation for college
 IV. College years
     A. Taking courses in preparation for career
     B. Becoming aware of the social pressures that will shape one's future
  V. Middle years
     A. Keeping abreast of developments in own profession
     B. Keeping posted on current events to be a responsible citizen
 VI. Retirement years
     A. Broadening knowledge through travel
     B. Reading books and periodicals so as not to lose touch with younger
        generation
Conclusion

_____

_____

_____

_____

_____

EXERCISE 10

Unity is one of the most important qualities of a good paragraph. Every idea in a paragraph should be related to a single topic, just as every topic should be related to the central idea suggested by the title. This exercise deals with the problem of *digression* (not sticking to the topic), which can to a greater or lesser degree destroy the unity of a paragraph. Study the outline carefully and draw a line through every idea that is not directly related to the central idea. In the space provided at the end of each division, write additional ideas drawn from your own experience or reading that further develop the thesis suggested by the title.

THE ADVANTAGES OF LIVING IN A METROPOLITAN AREA

Introduction
 I. Educational
    A. Generally higher quality of elementary schools and high schools
       1. Better equipment
       2. Better teachers
    B. Closer relationship between teacher and student in small towns
    C. Opportunity to attend college or university while living at home
    D. Variety of educational programs on noncommercial radio and TV
    E. Higher quality of newspapers to inform the citizens
    F. Fewer distractions in small towns, thus more opportunity to study

    B. Easy transportation
    F. More opportunity to gain extra, outside info

 II. Cultural
    A. Closer proximity to museums and other cultural centers
    B. Presence of local symphony orchestra and theater groups
    C. Greater opportunity in small town to associate with people of similar interests
    D. Many cultural activities in connection with municipal college or university
    E. More time in small town for those who want to belong to cultural group
    F. Appearance of outstanding personages in arts and sciences in big cities

C. Wide range of activities

III. Occupational
   A. Better opportunity to choose the type of job you want
   B. Better opportunity to choose the particular company you want to work for
   C. Better opportunity in small town to own your own business
   D. Larger size of company offers greater chance for promotion
   E. Lower cost of living in small town permits salary to go further
   F. Better opportunity to change jobs if you are dissatisfied

IV. Recreational
   A. Activities of social clubs such as American Legion and Elks better developed in small town
   B. Opportunity to see variety of professional entertainers in all fields
   C. Not necessary to travel to larger cities for entertainment
   D. Better opportunity for outdoor sports such as hunting and fishing in small town

EXERCISE 11

Emphasis in paragraphing (as in the total organization of a theme) refers to the systematic ordering of ideas and facts to stress their relative importance. One of the most common organizational patterns in writing is chronological. The main divisions of the following outline on the life of Abraham Lincoln are arranged according to this pattern. In developing the main divisions with specific details (from your own knowledge of American history or from reference books on Abraham Lincoln) you also are to arrange your material chronologically.

MY FAVORITE AMERICAN—ABRAHAM LINCOLN

Introduction

_____

_____

_____

_____

_____

   I. As a child in Kentucky

_____

_____

_____

_____

_____

   II. As a youth in Indiana

_____

_____

_____

_____

_____

III. As a young man in Salem, Illinois

_____

_____

_____

_____

_____

_____

IV. As a lawyer and politician in Springfield

_____

_____

_____

_____

_____

V. As President of the United States

_____

_____

_____

_____

_____

Conclusion

_____

_____

_____

_____

_____

EXERCISE 12

Coherence in paragraphing means making the ideas stick together. Although completeness, unity, and emphasis contribute greatly to coherence, the more specific way to achieve coherence is through the use of transitional words and phrases. The purpose of this exercise is to help you become more aware of transitional conjunctions and adverbial connectives in the hope that you will use more of them in your writing to make the logical relationships between your ideas clearer to the reader.

Consider the logical relationship between the parts of the sentence; then choose a word from one of the lists on page 54 and write it in the blank space.

Remember that in punctuating independent clauses a semicolon generally precedes the words from list IV. Also a comma is usually placed after the longer adverbial connectives. A comma usually precedes the conjunctions from lists I and III. Keeping these rules in mind and noting how the drill sentences are punctuated will help you to make the correct choice. In some cases two or more words from the lists can be used interchangeably.

1. You should be able to reach Birmingham by noon, ____*if*____ you do not run into a lot of traffic.

2. The weather this past weekend was ideal; ___*however*___, I did not have a chance to play golf.

3. We realized that a picnic table would be hard to find; ___*therefore*___ Joe and his wife agreed to leave for the park a couple of hours earlier than the rest of us to claim one.

4. We were forced to change our vacation plans, ____*after*____ the weatherman said a hurricane would probably strike the Florida coast on Saturday.

5. The teacher called on every student in the class; ___*thus*___ everyone had a chance to contribute to the discussion.

6. I had never tasted shrimp ____*until*____ I took a trip to New Orleans.

7. Gradually the spirits of the hikers began to brighten, ___*for*___ they knew that the end of the trail was near.

8. He seems to have the educational background to do the job; ___*moreover*___, he appears to have much enthusiasm and determination.

9. We finally decided to go to New York on our senior trip, ___*because*___ a majority of the students could not agree on any other destination.

10. I will study all the legal implications; _furthermore_____, I will interview the man who saw the accident before communicating with the insurance company.

11. The girls began to fix the picnic lunch, _while_____ the boys walked down to the lake to take a swim.

12. We realized that the roads would be dangerous over the holiday weekend; _Nevertheless____, we decided to make the trip to Indianapolis.

13. He was never too busy to stop and chat, _nor_____ did he hesitate to help us with our personal problems.

14. We decided never to eat in that restaurant again _although_____ we were absolutely starving.

15. He did not pass the English placement test; _consequently_, he will have to take the review English course.

Lesson 4

Logic

The person of ordinary intelligence in his everyday decisions frequently uses elementary logic, especially in weighing the causes and effects or the pros and cons of important matters that concern his personal life: in deciding whether or not to go to college, in choosing a college best suited to his abilities, in deciding on one job or another after he leaves college, in deciding to marry this or that boy or girl, in deciding whether to live in an apartment or to buy a house—the list could go on indefinitely. Thus logic in relation to writing is not an abstract principle that is foreign to your experience. But you can become more conscious of this mental process if a few basic terms and fallacies in logic that often limit the effectiveness of themes and reports are clearly defined.

Before the elementary fallacies that frequently appear in student writing are described, however, several important facts about language in general should be mentioned. (Of course, these comments will barely skim the surface.) Obviously language functions in several different ways. In a broad sense language can be separated into several different functions: logical, expressive, evocative, poetical, ceremonial, and mixed.

For example, a candidate for Congress, giving a political speech at a county fair on the Fourth of July, may be using language evocatively rather than logically if he makes this statement:

> My fellow citizens, I give you my solemn promise that if I am elected to Congress your income tax will be substantially reduced, and you will receive much higher subsidies for *not* raising corn. Moreover, upon my word of honor, I will use the high prestige of my elected office to influence the members of the Atomic Energy Commission to erect the proposed billion dollar atom smasher in this our beloved county.

A candidate for Congress who uses language in such a way is apparently playing fast and loose with truth, addressing his remarks to the gullible and naive for the purpose of gaining votes. He is using language evocatively rather than logically.

On the other hand, if you are required to write a reference paper in one of your college courses, you will be expected to use language in a logical—not an evocative—manner, the deeper purpose of your essay being the investigation and advancement of truth in the scientific sense of the word as defined by the brilliant logician, Thomas Aquinas: "For the nature of the true consists in a conformity of thing and intellect. . . . And the judgment is said to be true when it conforms to external reality."

One of the assumptions that the experienced reader makes even before he begins to read a serious essay is that the writer sincerely believes what he is saying. He is not consciously distorting reality for some hidden reason unknown to the reader.

However, the reader does not expect the writer, even though he is a professional, to reach irrefutable conclusions. For most essays are written on controversial topics; some of the conclusions like some of the basic assumptions will likely be educated opinions. Thus your composition may be successful even though you reach conclusions that are contrary to those of the reader, providing your paper is logical and well written.

Although many people can think and speak and write effectively even though they have not studied logic, your ability to write with precision and to make your assumptions and conclusions conform more closely with the truth of external reality should improve if you apply a few basic rules of this discipline, especially if you avoid logical fallacies.

One of the basic tools of logical thought—outlining—has already been discussed in detail. If you still do not realize the importance of this skill and have not made a determined effort to master its techniques (it is not as simple and easy as most students think), reread the first section. For no writing technique is quite so important to the inexperienced writer as formulating a coordinate outline before he begins his theme or report. Problems in logic can often be traced to poor organization; the person writes before he thinks clearly; thus he often makes hasty or unqualified generalizations. Using a three-level outline even for short themes will help you to avoid some of the serious fallacies that occur in student writing.

Unqualified or Hasty Generalization

This fallacy is the most common one in scholastic as well as professional writing. Maybe one reason is that some students have the mistaken notion that their writing will be most effective if they express their ideas in strong language in the tone of a rabble-rouser. A dogmatic tone in college exposition is usually a liability rather than a help. Furthermore, some students assume an all-knowing attitude, while the content and mechanics of their writing may not indicate brilliance. Before a student can solve his problem in faulty logic, of course, he must admit to himself that he is capable of fallacious thinking. The student who is anxious to improve the quality of his writing would do well to remind himself that he might make a gross error in logic, especially if he does not express his ideas in precise language. And, finally, students are prone to use too many all-inclusive words such as *good* and *bad, always* and *never, everyone* and *nobody.*

In defining a fallacy, such as unqualified generalization, it is difficult to make a clear-cut distinction between cause and effect. But for the purpose of analyzing the examples that follow and as a simple guide to help you spot this fallacy in your own writing, the following definition should suffice: A *hasty* or *unqualified generalization* is a statement that is imprecise or false because the writer (1) does not qualify an all-inclusive word such as *everyone,* (2) makes a dogmatic assertion that is mainly a personal opinion, (3) makes a positive assertion that is only partly true, or (4) makes an unqualified assertion based on stereotyped or emotional thinking rather than verifiable facts. The following examples and comments should give you a clearer understanding of this common fallacy.

Unqualified Generalization	Everyone should get plenty of exercise.
Improved	Adults as well as children should exercise regularly, unless, of course, they have a disability that makes exercise dangerous to their health.
Comment	In the poor example the writer has made a sweeping generalization that does not square with external reality; in other words, the statement is false. For certain individuals, strenuous exercise could be fatal, but this fact is not implied in the unqualified generalization.
Hasty Generalization	A good personality is the most important trait a person can have.
Improved	A pleasing personality is a valuable asset to an individual in almost everything he does.
Comment	The poor example is not only awkwardly phrased but also illogically conceived. Inasmuch as this judgment does not square with the opinion held by most intelligent people, the writer would have to clearly indicate that it is his personal opinion and not the consensus of the majority.
Unqualified Generalization	The Negroes believe the only way to express their thoughts is through race riots and freedom marches.
Improved	A large percentage of Negroes apparently believe that organized

	demonstrations are the best means of registering protests against discrimination.
Comment	From the way in which the poor example is stated, a careless reader might conclude that all Negroes hold such a view, when, as a matter of fact, a large percentage of the Negro population is opposed to race riots. The writer, then, has failed to qualify his generalization and has thus committed a fallacy.
Hasty Generalization	We fought in Korea to decide what form of government should rule the world: democracy or communism.
Improved	I believe that the intervention of the United Nations forces in Korea was necessary to stop Communist expansion; otherwise, most of the uncommitted nations of the world might have embraced communism and rejected democracy as their form of government.
Comment	The poor example represents the type of fuzzy thinking that is commonly found in student themes. Perhaps if the writer had imagined he was writing his essay to be read by a student in a Russian university, he would have been more precise in stating his ideas.

Post Hoc (After the Fact; Therefore, Because of the Fact)

Although this fallacy—apart from actual discourse—may seem too obvious for serious thought, it is one that occurs quite often in argument and persuasion, especially in the discussion of controversial issues such as religion and politics. A writer commits the *post hoc* fallacy when he illogically assumes a cause for an effect simply because the cause precedes the effect in time, as found in the examples that follow:

Post Hoc	Let's not take a trip to St. Louis, for every time we do it rains.
Post Hoc	Mr. Jones took a trip to France. While he was there he had a heart attack and died. Therefore, his trip to France caused his death.

Argumentum Ad Hominem (Discrediting a Person Associated with the Issue Rather Than the Issue Itself)

We commit the *argumentum ad hominem* fallacy when we attempt to disprove a proposition not by discussing the issues but by discrediting the person who made the proposal. This fallacy frequently appears in political writing and in arguments for or against religious beliefs or doctrines. The *argumentum ad hominem* may be effective in writing political propaganda, but if you use it in college exposition you leave yourself open to adverse criticism. Therefore, in discussing controversial topics, stick to the issues and avoid digressive character attacks on persons unless such an approach is logically sound.

Argumentum ad hominem	The theories of Karl Marx are obviously immoral and detrimental to the welfare of mankind, because he failed miserably to provide a decent living for his own family.
Comment	Attacking Karl Marx as an individual will probably weaken rather than strengthen your argument if you are trying to convince an intelligent reader that communism is a bad form of government. In discussing such a controversial topic, as we suggested earlier, your best approach is to present as many published historical facts as you can muster and try to avoid statements that give the impression of personal opinions.
Argumentum ad hominem	Inasmuch as Freud was an atheist, his therapeutic methods have little value in treating nervous disorders.
Comment	The logical fallacy in this statement is not quite as clear-cut as the previous one, for it contains certain implied premises that might strengthen the argument. But as it stands, the intelligent reader would probably reject it, because psychology as such is only tangentially related to religion; and a non-religious doctor, logically, could develop techniques for treating nervous disorders that would be effective for the believer as well as the atheist.

Begging the Question (Saying More or Less the Same Thing in the Beginning That You Say in the End)

Begging the question is another common fallacy in logic that is found in expository writing. (Perhaps it is often found in student writing because the writer is more concerned about words to fulfill the length requirement of the assignment than in the substance of his ideas.) In brief, you *beg the question* when you say more or less the same thing in the premise as you say in the conclusion:

> The belief in honesty is universal, for everyone believes in honesty.

> Helping our fellowmen is praiseworthy, because it deserves the approval of all.

You can avoid this fallacy by presenting more concrete facts and examples and by using more transitional words to emphasize the logical relationship between clauses in compound sentences—for example, *hence, thus, so, consequently, therefore,* etc.

False or Imperfect Analogy (Comparing Unlike Things That Have Implied Similarities)

An *analogy* is a figurative or metaphorical contrast between things or concepts based not on an actual likeness but upon implied similarities that may be common to the things or ideas being compared, for instance, comparing the buttons on a coat to the coordinate elements of a sentence or comparing a single atom to the solar system.

The vivid use of analogy is an effective technique in writing; as the Chinese proverb suggests, "One picture [is] worth a thousand words." An analogy is admissible as evidence in inductive reasoning, if the conclusion is drawn from other documentation in addition to the analogy. Therefore, there is nothing wrong with using analogy in expository writing, as long as it is appropriate and the similarities between the things being compared are of greater significance than the differences. If the opposite is true, we have a *false* or *imperfect* analogy, which can seriously weaken the effectiveness of an argument or discourse. The two statements that follow are examples of this fallacy—a type of false reasoning that you should try to avoid in your own writing.

False Analogy Writing is a skill like bowling or playing tennis. A person becomes skillful in sports only through actual practice. Therefore, studying textbooks on writing is a waste of time.

False Analogy If a man has a new car, he should drive it. If a woman has a new dress, she should wear it. If a nation has a new ballistic missile, it should use it.

Improper Appeal to Authority

After you complete your basic courses in composition, most of your writing for other courses will be in the form of reference papers, usually on topics related to a special course. Although the success of these papers depends to a large degree on your skill in organizing and expressing your own opinions, a reference paper should give the impression of objectivity: You are digesting, summarizing, and quoting the published writings of authors, who, in varying degrees, are expected to be authorities on the topic of your paper. For the writing you will do in your advanced courses, you would be wise to study carefully this logical fallacy, *improper appeal to authority*—one that frequently occurs in reference papers and other such reports.

Who is considered an authority? This, of course, is not an easy question to answer; heated debates frequently take place in law courts to decide if a certain individual is qualified as an authority—say to pass judgment on the sanity of the defendant. So you can see the difficulty in offering a positive answer to this question. But in general, an authority is a recognized expert in a given field—a person who has not only the learning or skill but also the ability to communicate his knowledge to others. In baseball, for instance, Pee Wee Reese could be considered an authority, partly because he was an outstanding player for the Brooklyn and Los Angeles Dodgers but mainly because of his ability as a sportscaster. In psychology, Dr. Erich Fromm would be considered an authority, because he has not only practiced psychiatry but also written a number of highly regarded books on the subject. An authority, then, is a person who is proficient in a special field and articulate in communicating his knowledge to others.

We commit the *improper appeal to authority* fallacy by citing testimonies of persons or groups who are not qualified to be called authorities, becoming prejudiced rather than logical in our thinking; by appealing to an authority that may have been competent at one time but is no longer accepted because of a change in time or circumstances; or by appealing to an authority that may be legitimate in one field but not qualified to give expert advice in another.

<table>
<tr><td>Improper Appeal
to Authority</td><td>The building of a turnpike from Louisville to Cincinnati should be opposed, for the State Council of Christian Ministers at their recent convention voted unanimously that such a road would not be in the best interest of the citizens of Kentucky.</td></tr>
<tr><td>Improper Appeal
to Authority</td><td>The founders of the Republic were vigorously opposed to a strong Federal government; therefore, the bill now before the Senate to regulate interstate commerce should be rejected.</td></tr>
</table>

Non Sequitur (It Does Not Follow.)

The last logical fallacy that we shall discuss, *non sequitur* (it does not follow), frequently is found in student writing, probably because the writer has not organized his material beforehand and is not quite sure what he is trying to say or is not concentrating on his discourse. We commit the *non sequitur* fallacy when the conclusion of our statement does not logically follow from the premise or premises. For example, "John is a very handsome man. He is also poor. Therefore, he has obviously wasted his talents."

Everyone who has ever seen John may agree that he is handsome, and the fact that he recently took the bankrupt law may confirm the fact that he is poor, and those people who know John best may agree that he has wasted his talents. But the original assertion is illogical (a *non sequitur*) because the premises provide no *basis* for the conclusion. The following examples contain the same fallacy for the same reason; namely, the premises do not have a direct relationship to the conclusion.

<table>
<tr><td>Non Sequitur</td><td>The girl is neither beautiful nor intelligent; therefore, she must come from the slum section of the city.</td></tr>
<tr><td>Non Sequitur</td><td>Communism is the most effective form of government, for during World War II the Russian army did a masterful job in defeating the Germans.</td></tr>
<tr><td>Non Sequitur</td><td>Since the existence of the soul cannot be scientifically proved, scepticism is the beginning of wisdom.</td></tr>
<tr><td>Non Sequitur</td><td>One of the main goals of socialism is a wider distribution of consumer goods. Communism has this same goal. Therefore, socialism and communism are in essence the same.</td></tr>
</table>

Faulty logic is a more serious problem in writing than most composition students think; they do not realize that the content (the logical ordering of the parts and the originality and precision of the ideas and language) is as important as the mechanics (punctuation, spelling, grammar, etc.) By underestimating the *what* and overestimating the *how*, writers do not give proper consideration to the opposite side of a debatable question. They jump to a conclusion without giving sufficient evidence or reach a conclusion that is not justified by the premises. They use imprecise or inappropriate figures of speech and are grossly prejudiced in considering only their own feelings or beliefs. All these are errors of logic which can be eliminated to improve the content, as well as the style, of your compositions, helping you to achieve the objectivity and maturity expected of a college student in all his written assignments.

EXERCISE 13

Each of the following sentences contains a fallacy. Identify the fallacy by number from the following list, and place that number in the left-hand column opposite the sentence.

1. Unqualified or Hasty Generalization
2. *Post Hoc* (After the Fact; Therefore, Because of the Fact)
3. *Argumentum ad Hominem* (Discrediting the Individual Rather Than the Issue)
4. Begging the Question
5. False Analogy
6. Improper Appeal to Authority
7. *Non Sequitur* (It does not follow.)

_____ 1. One must reject the theories of Francis Bacon, for he was unscrupulous in matters of public trust.

_____ 2. Everyone knows that most of our creative thinking is done unconsciously.

_____ 3. Wars have been fought in the name of religion; therefore, religion is an evil and should be abolished.

_____ 4. One of the most destructive fires in the history of the city happened the day the rampaging river reached its crest; the flood, therefore, was responsible for this awful catastrophe.

_____ 5. A southern drawl is characteristic of the natives of Alabama, for many of the people who live in Alabama have a southern drawl.

_____ 6. Sororities and fraternities should be banned on all college campuses; for Woodrow Wilson—one of our greatest Presidents—was opposed to social organizations that practiced discrimination.

_____ 7. One cannot learn to swim by studying lessons in a book. One must go into the water and gain direct experience. Thus the study of psychology is a waste of time, for one must learn from experience.

_____ 8. The life of Henry Ford is the greatest success story in the history of business.

_____ 9. Since beautiful girls use Wishy-Washy Soap, the way to achieve irresistible beauty is to use this amazing cleansing agent.

_____ 10. The attitudes of the two men are completely different.

_____ 11. Twentieth-century literature has been greatly influenced by Freud and other anti-religious thinkers, for much contemporary literature shows this influence.

_____ 12. It is obvious that this bill will not help the displaced coal miners; for Senator Brown—the author of the bill—for many years has been against labor unions.

_____ 13. Man does not have free will, for psychologists have shown that man is the product of instincts and environment.

_____ 14. The desegregation bill is an affront to our American way of life, for it is favored by the Communist Party.

_____ 15. Juvenile delinquency is caused by poor housing conditions.

EXERCISE 14

Each of the following sentences contains a fallacy. Identify the fallacy by number from the following list and place that number in the left-hand column opposite the sentence.

1. Unqualified or Hasty Generalization
2. *Post Hoc* (After the Fact; Therefore, Because of the Fact)
3. *Argumentum ad Hominem* (Discrediting the Individual Rather Than the Issue)
4. Begging the Question
5. False Analogy
6. Improper Appeal to Authority
7. *Non Sequitur* (It does not follow.)

_____ 1. The proposed location of the zoo is ideal, since it is supported by the Christian Ministerial Association.

_____ 2. Swift's ideas cannot be sound, for he died insane.

_____ 3. Honesty is admirable, because it deserves the approval of everyone.

_____ 4. The author was friendly toward the Nazi Party during World War II; hence, his views on dream analysis must be rejected because of his anti-Semetic views.

_____ 5. The day after I took a walk through the woods I began to sneeze and cough. My cold, then, was caused by walking in the woods.

_____ 6. All wars are caused by economic conflicts.

_____ 7. Outstanding students receive high grades; therefore, the giving of high grades produces outstanding students.

_____ 8. The President's plan for solving the economic problems will not work, for before he was elected he failed in business himself.

_____ 9. An hour or so after I left the movies I began to sneeze; therefore, I caught my cold while attending the movies.

_____ 10. Socialized medicine is an evil, because it is advocated by the Russians.

_____ 11. Tom is a congenial fellow, because he is always friendly and agreeable.

_____ 12. Writers are impulsive and temperamental.

_____ 13. To think that wars can be abolished is silly, for wars have occurred through all recorded history.

_____ 14. If man is to achieve happiness and good health he must adhere closely to a regular routine, for one can easily imagine the chaos that would result if the planets did not follow regular orbits around the sun.

_____ 15. Before making a decision, one should have a complete understanding of the factors involved.

Lesson 5

Deadwood

A recurring problem in student writing is *deadwood*: needless and useless words, phrases, or sentences that impede the smooth flow of language. It has been said that efficiency is a mark of intelligence. Most assuredly the intelligent writer will strive to communicate his thoughts efficiently by pruning the dead branches and useless limbs that clutter his theme or report.

Deadwood in writing can be divided into two broad categories—branches and twigs in the form of words and phrases that clog the sentences and useless limbs in the form of whole paragraphs that are unrelated to the subject being developed. The latter type of deadwood (also called digression) can usually be traced to poor outlining. The writer in all probability has not methodically organized his ideas in logical sequence before composing the first draft of his theme. Consequently, whole paragraphs are improperly related to the central idea. Few writers can compose a good theme without an outline.

In this section, however, we are mainly concerned with unnecessary twigs and useless branches that clutter sentences and paragraphs. Perhaps the easiest way to solve this problem is to understand *why* deadwood is so common in writing. In studying the causes, you should recognize the difficulty of drawing a sharp distinction between *cause* and *effect* and allow for interrelated causes.

Deadwood may result if the writer fails to use pronouns in place of repeated noun constructions.

Poor The athletes who make up the swimming and track and tennis teams are usually very fond of their sport. For the athletes who participate in these sports as a general rule receive neither financial help nor recognition.

Better The athletes who make up the swimming, track, and tennis teams are usually very fond of their sport. As a general rule they receive neither financial help nor recognition.

Poor The Red Cross volunteers deserve a great deal of credit for the help they gave during the recent tornado. The Red Cross volunteers staffed the rescue centers that provided housing, food, and clothing for the victims of the disaster.

Better The Red Cross volunteers deserve a great deal of credit for the help they gave during the recent tornado. They staffed the rescue centers that provided housing, food, and clothing for the victims of the disaster.

Deadwood may result when modifiers are used that do not add to the meaning of the sentence.

Poor I had a *very* difficult time getting my car started.
Better I had a difficult time getting my car started.

Poor We *really* had a wonderful time at the dance.
Better We had a wonderful time at the dance.

Poor I am *surely* glad I learned to swim when I was a kid.
Better I am glad I learned to swim when I was a kid.

Poor I was not *actually* surprised when I heard Joan got the lead in the play.
Better I was not surprised when I heard Joan got the lead in the play.

Poor I was *merely* sitting in class, letting my mind wander, when the professor asked me to explain the principle.
Better I was sitting in the class, letting my mind wander, when the professor asked me to explain the principle.

Poor I was *simply* too tired to go to the dance after studying for the mid-term exams.
Better I was too tired to go to the dance after studying for the mid-term exams.

Deadwood may result from needless repetition before examples or illustrations.

Poor We had to sacrifice a great deal in order to win the district contest. Some of the sacrifices made were omitting a few lunches, study periods, and history classes.
Better We had to sacrifice a great deal to win the district contest, for example, study periods, history classes, and (most important) noonday lunch.

Poor The novel was outstanding for several reasons. One reason it was outstanding is that everything had a meaning and a place.
Better I thought the novel was outstanding because every element was logically related to the theme.

Deadwood may result when words and phrases are awkwardly inserted rather than implied.

> Poor   Huntsville is a very interesting town to live in because of the many interesting and varied people living there.
>
> Better   Because of its heterogeneous population, Huntsville is a fascinating place to live.
>
> Poor   One of the most difficult decisions I have ever made in my life is whether or not I should go to college after high school or not go to college after high school.
>
> Better   I had a difficult time deciding whether or not I should go to college after graduating from high school.

Deadwood may result when related ideas are expressed in more than one sentence.

> Poor   The theme or main idea of this short story was best brought out when the boy met a pretty girl about his age at the horse races. This girl that the boy met was in a higher class of society than he was.
>
> Better   The theme of the story became clear in the scene at the horse races, when the young man met an attractive girl who, apparently, was from a higher level of society than he.
>
> Poor   The students gave up their leisure time to sell magazines. Most of the people bought the magazines. Some who did not need magazines bought them just to help the class.
>
> Better   The students gave up their leisure time to sell magazines, and many people in the neighborhood bought them mainly to help a worthy cause.

You can see, then, by comparing the poor examples with the better ones, that the elimination of deadwood not only will improve the clarity of a sentence but will make it more readable. By avoiding redundant phrases and roundabout sentence patterns, your writing should be neater and more precise. However, deadwood is not as easy to spot as one might think. It is easy enough for a sharp reader to see the deadwood in another's writing; but it is difficult—unless you make a special effort—to see it in your own. Perhaps the easiest way to detect wordiness is to proofread your paper out loud, looking for words and phrases and even complete sentences that are nonessential. A good time to look for deadwood is just before you write the final draft of your theme.

EXERCISE 15

Rewrite the following sentences, eliminating the deadwood (1) by using a pronoun to take the place of a wordy noun construction, (2) by deleting nonessential modifiers, (3) by eliminating awkward repetition before examples, (4) by striking out implied words or phrases, (5) by combining the closely related thoughts of two or more sentences into one, or (6) by using any other method that seems practical. Before you begin the exercise, please study the following example.

> *Poor*   There are also many young people who can't afford to go to a school out of town.
>
> *Better* Many people cannot afford to attend an out-of-town college.

1. I vacationed one week in Milwaukee. In that city I stayed with my sister and her family.

_____

_____

2. I will be able to put my training to a very useful purpose in life.

_____

_____

3. A well-educated man is usually able to attain success.

_____

4. I believe every person on earth should have his or her chance to decide what kind of job or work to do.

_____

_____

5. I would like to say that I believe television could be an effective educational medium.

_____

_____

6. Upon returning back to our hotel, we took a nap and then dressed for dinner.

_____

_____

7. Eventually we reached Kingsville, Ontario, and enjoyed shopping around for souvenirs.

_____

_____

8. We were amazed at the vast expanse of water and the continuous roar of the breakers of the waves as they rolled in on the sparking white beach.

_____

_____

9. My best teacher was Mr. Hopkins. Mr. Hopkins taught physical education at Jefferson High School.

_____

_____

10. A well-educated man is a man who keeps well informed.

_____

11. My favorite teacher in school was Mr. Schuler.

_____

12. I believe television does foster maturity for the following reasons: television is informative, it is educational, and it is entertaining.

_____

_____

13. In conclusion I wish to say that I know how I got off on the wrong foot.

_____

_____

14. I would advise everybody who is an outdoor type of person to try fishing.

_____

_____

15. With all this leisure time the American has more time to do things around his home.

_____

_____

EXERCISE 16

Rewrite the following sentences, eliminating the deadwood (1) by using a pronoun to take the place of a wordy noun construction, (2) by deleting nonessential modifiers, (3) by eliminating awkward repetition before examples, (4) by striking out implied words or phrases, (5) by combining the closely related thoughts of two or more sentences into one, or (6) by using any other method that seems practical. Before you begin the exercise, study the following example.

> *Poor* One of the finest aspects that football helps to create in a person is the ability for a person to learn to get along with other types of people no matter who they are.
>
> *Better* Playing football helps a person to learn to get along with others.

1. A salesman must take the initiative on his own.

   _____

2. To me my work as an orderly is the most stimulating I have ever done.

   _____

   _____

3. In closing I can only say that in the future I hope to take a more active role in politics.

   _____

   _____

4. Henry Clay was an intelligent and vital type of person.

   _____

5. In conclusion, a liberal education isn't liberal unless it offers courses in the humanities.

   _____

   _____

6. In the novel there are two major conflicts that keep the plot moving. These two conflicts are the social insecurity of the hero and his religious doubts that stem from his agnostic education.

   _____

   _____

   _____

7. Miniature golf is a game that almost everyone can enjoy and everyone can play.

_____

_____

8. Helen Keller has dedicated her own life to the education of the blind.

_____

_____

9. We spent a total of fifteen hours on the train.

_____

10. The future of my life is as uncertain as the weather.

_____

11. Our train rolled through a countless number of cities and towns.

_____

_____

12. I think the summer months are the most enjoyable months of the year.

_____

_____

13. The time I learned my best lesson was the day I disturbed a swarm of bees in a tree.

_____

_____

14. I entered college in order to prepare myself for a teaching career.

_____

_____

15. A tourist in Paris can't see all the points of interest in a three- or four-day period of time.

_____

_____

EXERCISE 17

Rewrite the following sentences, eliminating the deadwood (1) by using a pronoun to take the place of a wordy noun construction, (2) by deleting nonessential modifiers, (3) by eliminating awkward repetition before examples, (4) by striking out implied words or phrases, (5) by combining the closely related thoughts of two or more sentences into one, or (6) by using any other method that seems practical. Before you begin the exercise, study the following example.

Poor   Many charts about the human anatomy are placed on the walls. These charts contain detailed information on our body.

Better   Many detailed charts on the human anatomy were placed on the walls.

1. The wind made the autumn leaves fall to the ground.

   _____

2. The furniture industry is one of the most highly competitive businesses there is.

   _____

   _____

3. There is nothing quite so breathtaking and alluring as the Grand Canyon to attract the eye of the sightseer.

   _____

   _____

4. Mr. Graham was the kind of man who didn't mind giving up some of his time to help the boys.

   _____

   _____

5. The wind and rain let up some the next day after what had been a very wet and rainy night.

   _____

   _____

6. Tornadoes and hurricanes are exceedingly dangerous storms, and one should take every safety precaution when warned of their approach.

   _____

   _____

7. Since a teacher is a person who guides and instructs young people, he should have an inquiring mind.

   _____

   _____

8. The subject of birth control, which is widely debated, is a very controversial subject.

   _____

   _____

9. Some individuals who were contacted remarked how useful buildings of this type would have been to them when they attended the college years ago.

   _____

   _____

   _____

10. A student may attend all of Professor Brown's classes during the course of the semester.

    _____

    _____

11. The simple language and sentences help clarify what the essay is about.

    _____

    _____

12. In several instances students find themselves with little extra time in which they have nothing to do.

    _____

    _____

13. All students were treated equally alike.

    _____

14. She was the type of teacher who showed no favoritism toward any of her students.

    _____

    _____

15. We read the essay with confused expressions on our faces.

    _____

    _____

EXERCISE 18

Rewrite the following sentences, eliminating the deadwood (1) by using a pronoun to take the place of a wordy noun construction, (2) by deleting nonessential modifiers, (3) by eliminating awkward repetition before examples, (4) by striking out implied words or phrases, (5) by combining the closely related thoughts of two or more sentences into one, or (6) by using any other method that seems practical. Before you begin the exercise, study the following example.

Poor   These improvements are things that all the people will benefit by.
Better   All the people will benefit by these improvements.

1. In conclusion I would like to say that I think I will gain much from college if I can learn to use my time wisely.

   _____

   _____

2. If a person has the characteristics of being sincere and honest, one can depend on him to do what he says.

   _____

   _____

3. Bill can do just about anything when he makes up his mind that he is going to do it.

   _____

   _____

4. Television does foster maturity in many ways. One of the ways in which television fosters maturity is in educational television.

   _____

   _____

5. We pooled our money together and bought an old car.

   _____

6. The sport football is one of my favorite pastimes.

   _____

7. The time I learned my best lesson was when I cut school.

   _____

8. The swarm of bees was about a foot wide, and it was about as long as a yardstick.

_____

_____

9. The college student must plan his time wisely. Also, a student in college must often make certain changes in his habits.

_____

_____

10. One of the requirements was a term paper. It was to consist of fifteen hundred words on a subject of our choice.

_____

_____

_____

11. In my opinion learning to adapt myself to college life is my biggest problem.

_____

_____

12. She is an expert in the field of medical technology.

_____

13. I have had some teachers who would give the class I was in tests on material that we had never before covered in class.

_____

_____

14. A raincoat should be so designed to protect the individual who wears it.

_____

_____

15. The novel had many outstanding qualities. These outstanding qualities were all part of the author's genius in creating a literary masterpiece.

_____

_____

_____

EXERCISE 19

Rewrite the following sentences, eliminating the deadwood (1) by using a pronoun to take the place of a wordy noun construction, (2) by deleting nonessential modifiers, (3) by eliminating awkward repetition before examples, (4) by striking out implied words or phrases, (5) by combining the closely related thoughts of two or more sentences into one, or (6) by using any other method that seems practical. Before you begin the exercise, study the following example.

> *Poor*   But rich people are unhappy at times just as the average person finds himself not too happy at times.
>
> *Better* But rich people—just like ordinary people—are not always happy.

1. Some people have made the claim that the violence one can see on TV is the main cause for the rise of juvenile delinquency that exists in the world today.

   _____

   _____

   _____

2. Weather reports ahead of time give us an idea of what to expect as far as the weather.

   _____

   _____

3. A quality most important in teaching to me is a knowledge of the subject being taught.

   _____

   _____

4. Her honeymoon tour which lasted a duration of six months was nothing but a total bore to her.

   _____

   _____

5. Another beautiful spot which I visited was Crystal Lake which is located at the end of Mountain Ridge Road.

   _____

   _____

6. One of the classes he taught was typing which was the first class I had under him.

_____

_____

7. I like to take pictures and later relive my trip over again.

_____

8. It has long been a fact that travel is perhaps one of the best means of broadening a person intellectually.

_____

_____

9. My best teacher made his classes interesting to the students.

_____

10. We had a considerable amount of spare time.

_____

11. First of all let me say that both these men were almost identical in the way they lived.

_____

12. I took part in two types of recreation. One was water skiing. Another was horseback riding.

_____

_____

13. I have decided to improve my knowledge of the English language.

_____

14. As of yet I have made no definite plans as to what I shall do with my unoccupied or spare time.

_____

_____

15. As far as my personal opinion goes I like classical music better than popular.

_____

_____

EXERCISE 20

Rewrite the following sentences, eliminating the deadwood (1) by using a pronoun to take the place of a wordy noun construction, (2) by deleting nonessential modifiers, (3) by eliminating awkward repetition before examples, (4) by striking out implied words or phrases, (5) by combining the closely related thoughts of two or more sentences into one, or (6) by using any other method that seems practical. Before you begin the exercise, study the following example.

Poor   Several qualities of *West Side Story* show why it was an outstanding movie. Three of these qualities are acting, photography, and choreography.

Better   The superb acting, excellent photography, and unique choreography made *West Side Story* an outstanding movie.

1. After my instructions on what to do I made an attempt to land the plane.

   _____

2. This hurricane, whose name was Flora, was the worst hurricane to hit New Jersey in twenty years.

   _____

   _____

3. But they never stop to realize just what lies ahead in the future.

   _____

4. A few years ago we had a very long cold spell which froze all the ponds with ice.

   _____

   _____

5. Some of the great dramas of all time are shown on television from time to time.

   _____

6. Man ponders in his mind both doubts and fears about life.

   _____

7. A career in the navy has both advantages and disadvantages. The return to civilian life from the military also has advantages and disadvantages.

   _____

   _____

8. I had to decide whether to settle for an average living or to set a higher goal for myself.

   _____

9. Sunday night is when we have little get-togethers that bring out the real leaders of the church.

   _____

   _____

10. While in New York I visited many interesting places. Some of them were the Empire State Building, the Statue of Liberty, and the Radio City Music Hall.

    _____

    _____

11. At some time in most girls' lives, they must make a decision whether to embark upon a career in the business world or a career in marriage.

    _____

    _____

12. The major decision in my life which I contributed the most thought to, perhaps, is the decision of what I wanted to do with my life after graduating from high school.

    _____

    _____

13. Davis University offers a variety of different subjects for the student, including foreign languages.

    _____

14. The climate would be considered mostly mild in the summer, with an average temperature of 80 degrees.

    _____

    _____

15. Since the beginning of time humanity has passed through many periods of progress. Some of these were: the Stone Age, the Iron Age, the Industrial Age, and the Atomic Age.

    _____

    _____

Lesson 6

Inflated Diction

The term *inflated diction* as used in this discussion means awkward, unnatural, flowery, pretentious, or overly formal writing, as exemplified by the following sentences:

Inflated Diction   Unimpeachable integrity in our business dealings with others will produce results of a more substantial nature.

Inflated Diction   Insofar as hesitation may incapacitate my progression, it creates my biggest problem.

Inflated Diction   The undesirables abide in neighborhoods befitting their position of social retardation.

Why do students write such abominable sentences? Primarily, we assume, because they are trying to impress the reader, failing to realize that he does not enjoy the backtracking and hair-pulling that is needed to understand this type of jargon. Therefore, your writing in all probability will be more effective if you make a conscious effort to avoid fine writing and develop a style that is more in keeping with your speech patterns. If you detect inflated diction in your composition and want to revise it, ask yourself this question, "How would I express this idea in speech?" Take another look at the above examples. Don't you agree that the following revisions show a definite improvement in clarity as well as in style?

> *Better*   Honesty is the best policy.
> *Better*   Hesitation is my biggest problem, because it impedes my progress.
> *Better*   The bums and petty thieves often live in the slums of big cities.

In stressing the close relationship between conversation and writing, we do not mean to imply that they are the same. If you were sitting at a table in the student lounge with several of your friends, having a cup of coffee and a little friendly chit-chat, and if one of the boys or girls had a small recorder hidden in his pocket or in her purse and got the bull session down on tape and later transcribed it on paper, you might note certain things about the conversation that we should try to avoid in writing.

1. The speakers will jump from one topic to another; we expect writing to be better organized than speech.
2. The speakers will use many short, simple sentences; we expect the sentence patterns in writing to be more compact, using more complex and compound sentences.
3. The speakers' sentences will contain much deadwood; we expect the writer to prune the deadwood from his total composition and sentences.
4. The language of the speakers—unless they are exceptional—will be studded with colloquial expressions and clichés (matters that we shall discuss in subsequent sections of this book), which are frowned upon in written composition.

Informal speech, quite naturally, will differ from careful writing for at least two reasons. In conversation the person often says the first thing that comes to his mind in order to avoid long pauses or awkward stammering. The writer, on the other hand, can in one sense stop time while he searches his mind for the precise word or phrase. Yet of even greater importance, the impromptu speaker must outline the pattern of his thoughts in his head on the spur of the moment, while the writer can (and should) spend considerable time arranging his ideas and facts before he composes the first draft of his essay. So it is not unreasonable to expect writing to be a more effective form of communication than unplanned conversation.

However, such a pat conclusion is sometimes misleading, for many people (maybe most people) can speak better than they can write. To avoid inflated diction in your writing, make a conscious effort to make your writing conform more to your speech patterns. The primary cause of inflated diction is probably a misguided attempt to achieve a literary effect. However, we should like to pinpoint a few more specific causes that may help you to understand and overcome this problem.

Deadwood

In getting rid of the deadwood you may at the same time eliminate the inflated diction.

Poor   The subject of teen-age marriages is a topic which could create a magnitude of controversial arguments.

Better   The pros and cons of teen-age marriages have been widely debated.

Poor   When I have attained the goal of my desire, there will be even greater understanding between us.

Better   After I have reached my goal, we should understand each other better.

Poor   I found that establishing myself a budget was the only way to manage profitably on a small income.

Better   Adhering to a budget was the only way I could manage on a small income.

Cloudy thinking

Clarity is one of the most important qualities of good expository writing. Inflated diction often acts as a smoke screen to obscure your precise meaning.

Poor   Mr. Kelly could present his subject with a persuasive attitude.

Better   Mr. Kelly was a very persuasive salesman.

Poor   He dealt with the students on an equal basis of intelligence.

Better   He did not talk down to his students.

Poor   In the play the hero is described as a character of perfection.

Better   In the play the hero is portrayed as a perfectionist, a rather neurotic man who could not tolerate the faults of others.

Awkward use of passive voice

There is nothing inherently wrong in using the passive voice; in fact, sometimes it is preferred over the active voice. But the latter is more effective where the subject needs to be stressed.

Poor   This tournament had long been awaited by me.

Better   For weeks I had looked forward to the tournament.

Poor   Card playing, reading, and eating soon began.

Better   Soon we began to talk, play cards, and read.

Poor   We took an early train and Nashville was reached around five.

Better   We took an early train and reached Nashville around five.

Putting the cart before the horse

Our intrinsic sense of logic or sense of proportion will help us to put first things first.

Poor   Realism is the main reason that the story is my favorite.

Better   The story is my favorite because of its unique realism.

Poor   The pronounced characteristics of this outstanding movie were excellent photography, fine acting, and realism.

Better	The movie was outstanding because of its excellent photography, convincing acting, and stark realism.
Poor	Organization is one of the better ways to have a successful program.
Better	A successful program usually depends upon advance planning.

Awkward use of negative

Using too many negative words often results in awkward as well as vague statements. Hence, it is a good idea to heed the advice of a song that was popular some years ago, "Accentuate the positive—eliminate the negative."

Poor	It is not seldom that we find hate as a characteristic of belligerent people.
Better	Belligerent people are often filled with hate.
Poor	The unconscious mind plays an unnegligible role in man's life.
Better	The unconscious mind plays an important role in the life of man.
Poor	Mr. Moore's teaching methods were not subordinate to his attitude and personality.
Better	Besides being a first-rate teacher, Mr. Moore had a friendly personality and an optimistic view of life.

Euphemism

This is an uncommon term, so perhaps we should consult the dictionaries for a precise meaning. (*Webster's New World Dictionary:* Euphemism—"A word or phrase that is less expressive or direct but considered less distasteful, less offensive, etc. than another." Funk & Wagnalls *Standard College Dictionary:* Euphemism—"Substitution of a mild or roundabout word or expression for another felt to be too blunt or otherwise distasteful or painful.")

The etiquette of formal composition—the type of writing that you will generally be called upon to do in college—assumes that you will use discretion in the choice of your words; yet there is a danger of being too polite (as the following examples will show) and ending up with a lifeless euphemism.

Poor	Since my financial status was small, I decided to attend the state university.
Better	Since I didn't have much money, I decided to attend the state university.
Poor	Public opinion of him was very low.
Better	Most people disliked him intensely.
Poor	By then he will be of an age that he will not enjoy his money.
Better	By then he will be too old to enjoy his money.

Inflated diction, then, as you can see from the examples that we have given, detracts from the clarity and force of your writing. Ironically, you should view with suspicion any sentences of which you are inordinately proud, for usually these are the very sentences that seem inflated and pretentious to the reader.

Having decided that a sentence is inflated and wishing to revise it, ask yourself two important questions: (1) How would I express this idea in speech? (2) Can I express this idea in more concrete language that will be clearer to the reader? If you put yourself in the place of the reader and organize and write your theme with that relationship in mind, you will try to make your theme as clear and readable as possible.

EXERCISE 21

Rewrite the following sentences, using language more in keeping with ordinary speech patterns. Two pertinent questions may help you to improve these sentences: (1) How would I express this idea in speech? (2) Can I express this idea in more concrete language that will be clearer to the reader? Consider the following poor and better examples before doing the exercise.

> *Poor* Why isn't there individuality when facing the question of smoking and drinking?
>
> *Better* Why do most teen-agers follow the crowd when it comes to drinking and smoking?

1. Several months ago industry moved to my town under the name of General Electric.

_____

_____

2. When I was of an early age my parents would not let me have any responsibilities.

_____

_____

3. My present occupation is a farmer.

_____

4. They often try to discuss subjects above their category and usually make a fool of themselves.

_____

_____

5. The varied autumn colors are a beauty to see.

_____

6. In the farmer is a sense of accomplishment.

_____

7. I found that the students from big cities are more adept to learning than I.

_____

_____

8. Since farming prosperity has declined sharply, the economy of our country has gone into a decline.

_____

_____

9. Show me a large production city that does not have a displeasing odor.

_____

_____

10. In a small town friends develop quickly.

_____

11. The world today is in a serious condition with the threat of atomic war present.

_____

_____

12. The thought of disciplining myself came into existence.

_____

13. For me the result of going too fast was a traffic fine.

_____

14. The financial end is better for a man who has a college education.

_____

_____

15. Being dishonest will dwell on your conscience.

_____

EXERCISE 22

Rewrite the following sentences, using language more in keeping with ordinary speech patterns.

Two pertinent questions may help you to improve these sentences: (1) How would I express this idea in speech? (2) Can I express this idea in more concrete language that will be clearer to the reader? Consider the following poor and better examples before doing the exercise.

> *Poor* The mood set can be classified as one with restless and weird aspects.
> *Better* The incessant rain and the banging of the shutter against the casement, evoked a mood of weird restlessness.

1. One of the major tasks of any individual is to find some field of income which satisfies his needs.

_____

_____

2. After failing in scholastic training, he got a job in Richmond as an editor.

_____

_____

3. If a person doesn't enjoy working with young people, he should not enter the field of teaching.

_____

_____

4. Man needs to be associated with a particular group, society-wise, or his life is made miserable.

_____

_____

5. He was possessed with many responsibilities.

_____

6. When he returned he found that his financial status was in a very bad condition.

_____

_____

7. An outstanding personality was another trait of my teacher.

_____

8. Future employment is greatly dependent on how I do in college.

_____

_____

9. This job, though unsatisfactory to his desires, allowed him time to work on his mathematical theories.

_____

_____

10. The year I spent in Mr. Scott's class was the year I gained my biggest share of knowledge in English grammar.

_____

_____

11. These cartoon strips created a comedy effect on the American public.

_____

_____

12. He never will be a figure of perfection.

_____

13. The situation rendered it necessary to be less extravagant with money.

_____

_____

14. I gained certain concepts of information which I believe are vital to every freshman.

_____

_____

15. When women marry they assume the responsibility of overseeing the maintenance of the household.

_____

_____

EXERCISE 23

Rewrite the following sentences, using language more in keeping with ordinary speech patterns.

Two pertinent questions may help you to improve these sentences: (1) How would I express this idea in speech? (2) Can I express this idea in more concrete language that will be clearer to the reader? Consider the following poor and better examples before doing the exercise.

> *Poor*   "The Lagoon," written by Joseph Conrad, is a story possessing extraordinary elements of style and characterization.
>
> *Better*   "The Lagoon" by Joseph Conrad is outstanding because of its rich style and vivid characterization.

1. The bridge is the one sight along the highway that remains in memory.

   _____

2. It was to the largest of these caves that we made our way through the dense underbrush.

   _____

   _____

3. Scholastic and social values are important subjects of discussion when considering the controversial issues based on the college cooperative program.

   _____

   _____

4. His style of clothing fits the modern trend.

   _____

5. The student is faced with many problems related to the interference of his line of concentration.

   _____

   _____

6. Although I could detect the introvertive aspect through her speech, I also discovered that she had many energy disposing facets.

   _____

   _____

7. The typical rowdiness of boys at this age did not seem to show in Bob.

   _____

8. In visiting Mt. Vesuvius, the volcano offers a person views of wondrous beauty and unexpected thrills.

   _____

   _____

9. My first impression of Mr. Jones seems to be a true and lasting evaluation.

   _____

   _____

10. Watering the lawn or doing other such chores, faded blue jeans, a ragged shirt, and sloppy, worn-out shoes make up his apparel.

    _____

    _____

    _____

11. It is possible that I was not exposed to the true natives everywhere I went.

    _____

    _____

12. Her warm personality and marvelous sense of humor filled her classroom with a pleasant environment.

    _____

    _____

13. The intelligence of this teacher did not just pertain to his particular field.

    _____

    _____

14. Much of the admiration held by people for Mr. London was the result of bravery.

    _____

    _____

15. He can talk to his students so each of them finds a personal identification with what he is saying.

    _____

    _____

EXERCISE 24

Rewrite the following sentences using language more in keeping with ordinary speech patterns.

Two pertinent questions may help you to improve these sentences: (1) How would I express this idea in speech? (2) Can I express this idea in more concrete language that will be clearer to the reader? Consider the following poor and better examples before doing the exercise.

Poor A controversial figure would be an excellent description of Lawrence of Arabia.

Better Lawrence of Arabia was indeed a controversial figure.

1. Another important phase of this sport is to find another person who also likes activities of this type.

   _____

   _____

2. Helping others who are in need of help is a trait that distinguishes a person who is interested in the welfare of the people whom he associates with.

   _____

   _____

   _____

3. All the things that passed through my mind during the flight would be hard to recapitulate.

   _____

   _____

4. The force with which the rain was coming down was very rapid.

   _____

5. I have not been appreciative of Shakespeare's works.

   _____

6. Many things of a festive nature are running through my mind as to the nature of plans or places I would like to visit over the Thanksgiving weekend.

   _____

   _____

   _____

7. Now that you have reached the college era a sense of individualism should be prevalent.

_____

_____

8. I find that my speed in reading varies with the thought contained in the sentence.

_____

_____

9. As I began to advance in years I found myself to be inclined toward solving difficult problems.

_____

_____

10. Everyone is hoping to achieve the victory.

_____

11. Compliments to all were favorable and plentiful.

_____

12. Superficially Miss Brown seemed very distant, but once acquainted with her she was very warm and human.

_____

_____

13. Seat belts were fastened as we descended at the airport.

_____

_____

14. The lounges are of antique furnishing with deep soft carpets covering the floors.

_____

_____

15. As an individual, his characteristic behavior was well organized.

_____

_____

EXERCISE 25

Rewrite the following sentences using language more in keeping with ordinary speech patterns.

Two pertinent questions may help you to improve these sentences: (1) How would I express this idea in speech? (2) Can I express this idea in more concrete language that will be clearer to the reader? Consider the following poor and better examples before doing the exercise.

Poor The play was unique in the manner that a serious atmosphere and humorous tinge were intermingled.

Better The subtle blending of humor and sadness made the play unique.

1. The music of *My Fair Lady* was definitely one of the successful factors of the movie.

_____

_____

2. Tension prevails as the discussion of money arises.

_____

3. Not infrequently the demonstrators were arrested.

_____

4. Mr. Perry maintained a concept of teaching that fundamentally resulted in treating the entire class as an entity when discipline or favors were the concern of a particular matter.

_____

_____

5. Money is usually the first aspect of any endeavor to be examined.

_____

6. Drama programs give us a conception of what psychological problems exist in our environment.

_____

7. Skill was not possessed by those on whom the cameras were directed.

_____

8. Not infrequently inattention becomes a major problem.

_____

9. A resentment against Lincoln High School was prevalent at Eastern High School.

_____

_____

10. Recreation is sought on the golf courses and tennis courts.

_____

11. Physically he is described as a man; however, we become aware that he still retains the immaturity of an adolescent.

_____

_____

12. The not unsubstantial number who were against the measure caused it to be rejected.

_____

_____

13. I felt the opportunity for more money was to be had as a civilian.

_____

14. In retrospect of the observations presented herein one may conclude that the story failed to communicate the author's meaning.

_____

_____

15. Certain concepts pertaining to the importance of occupations should be examined by young people.

_____

_____

EXERCISE 26

Rewrite the following sentences using language more in keeping with ordinary speech patterns.

Two pertinent questions may help you to improve these sentences: (1) How would I express this idea in speech? (2) Can I express this idea in more concrete language that will be clearer to the reader? Consider the following poor and better examples before doing the exercise.

Poor   Another contribution to the decline in individualism is people's personal appearance.

Better It is difficult to say which comes first: conformity in appearance or monkey-like thinking.

1. Most of the students have an adequate vocabulary and a knowing attitude.

   _____

2. My feeling toward the foreign movies is one of approval.

   _____

3. Advertisements help a person in decisions on products to use in the home.

   _____

   _____

4. The value of TV has been debated since it was first made a public feature.

   _____

   _____

5. Some students find it difficult to keep a steady pace of involvement in a single area.

   _____

   _____

6. Intercollegiate athletics should play a part which is second to the aspect of academic education.

   _____

   _____

7. The wrong kind of TV shows may disrupt our moral attitude.

   _____

8. Humorous would be a descriptive word for him.

_____

9. The talents and personality of my high school teacher were of such a dynamic proportion that he vividly stands out in my mind.

_____

_____

10. He developed a high degree of communication between himself and the reader.

_____

_____

11. The most outstanding feature of St. Peter's Cathedral is the monstrosity of its size.

_____

_____

12. Through his guidance and instruction he gave me an ample background for college.

_____

_____

13. I have participated in baseball since I was nine.

_____

14. Television has its discrepancies.

_____

15. I believe that the percentage of teen-agers with high moral standards is relatively higher than the percentage with low moral standards.

_____

_____

Lesson 7

Weak Words

A sharp distinction between weak and dynamic words or overemphatic and precise words is difficult to make, for the context in which you are writing to a large extent determines (or should determine) the vocabulary you use. For instance, in a letter to a friend or a theme about your personal experience, you may deliberately use general and exaggerated words to achieve a humorous or ironic effect, and this light and unpretentious style may make your letter or essay readable and entertaining.

But most of the writing you do in college and the letters and reports you will write after you leave college will require a more exact vocabulary than does a breezy letter to your buddy in the Navy. The success or failure of the former depends largely on their precision and clarity. Also as you advance in college your written assignments more and more are based on the books and periodicals related to a given course, and the standards of judging the truth or falsity of these reports become more absolute.

The same high standards will apply to the writing you will do after you leave college. As a sales executive you may or may not get the order because of the quality of your correspondence. As a certified public accountant you may retain or lose a client because of the sharpness or dullness of your audit report. As a laboratory scientist your lengthy report based on months of research may be accepted or rejected because of the precision or vagueness of the language. In most practical writing situations clarity and exactness in diction are important, for before the reader can judge the merit of your conclusions, he must have a clear understanding of what you are saying. Thus in advising you to eliminate weak and overemphatic words from your writing and to substitute more concrete and precise words, we are referring to a particular type of writing—the more formal essays and reports you will have to do in school and the letters and reports that you will have to compose in your professional work.

The clarity of your writing depends to a large extent on the use of concrete words rather than abstract or general ones that have lost their vigor because of overuse. Here are some of the words that are considered weak: *awful, bad, beautiful, big, fine, funny, good, grand, great, interesting, lovely, nice, pretty, real, sure, swell, things, very, wonderful.* You can add others to the list once you have formed the habit of looking for weak words in your writing.

Although the distinction between weak and overemphatic words is sometimes a matter of opinion, *weak* words generally dull the sharpness and incisiveness of writing by not saying enough, while *overemphatic* words distort the impression by saying more than is called for. The following words—and you can add others to the list—are often too strong or too emotional for standard expository writing: *amazing, ancient, fabulous, magnificent, perfect, splendid, terrific, tremendous.*

Considering the many rules that may confuse rather than help, you should decide for yourself if this is one of the need-to-know or nice-to-know fundamentals that is worth following or disregarding. Before you make up your mind, though, we ask that you give this principle a fair day in court by studying the poor and better examples in which we have substituted more precise words for the weak ones and more moderate ones for those marked overemphatic. We believe you will agree that the revised sentences are better and that your writing too will improve if you employ this technique.

Poor	I enjoyed studying the *interesting* paintings at the Museum of Modern Art.
Better	I enjoyed studying the *unique* paintings at the Museum of Modern Art.
Poor	Senator Conner discussed many *things* in his television address to the nation.
Better	Senator Conner discussed many *issues* in his television address to the nation.
Poor	Dr. Eady had a *good* reason for not attending the committee meeting.
Better	Dr. Eady had a *valid* reason for not attending the committee meeting.
Poor	The *bad* snowstorm prevented the trains from running on schedule.
Better	The *severe* snowstorm prevented the trains from running on schedule.
Poor	I received a *nice* letter from my high school principal, wishing me success in college.
Better	I received a *friendly* letter from my high school principal, wishing me success in college.

Poor	I felt *fine* after my long hike through the country.
Better	I felt *invigorated* after my long hike through the country.
Poor	The county agent gave a *magnificent* talk on the necessity for crop rotation.
Better	The county agent gave an *informative* talk on the necessity for crop rotation.
Poor	Joan felt *awful,* so she decided not to go to class.
Better	Joan felt *nauseated,* so she decided not to go to class.
Poor	Dean Crutcher was well liked by the students because of his *wonderful* sense of humor.
Better	Dean Crutcher was well liked by the students because of his *warm* sense of humor.
Poor	Tom felt *great* after he received an A on the history test.
Better	Tom felt *elated* after he received an A on the history test.
Poor	I was *amazed* at the difference I found between high school and college.
Better	I was *surprised* at the difference I found between high school and college.
Poor	Although Dorothy Dean sings mostly popular songs, she has a *splendid* voice.
Better	Although Dorothy Dean sings mostly popular songs, she has a *well-trained* voice.

The difference between *poor, average,* and *superior* themes is determined to a large degree by the suitability and precision of the language. Thus the first-rate writer usually has an extensive vocabulary, although he does not try to flaunt it by using the big word when the common word is more to the point.

The words that we have labeled *weak* and *overemphatic* are used frequently by practiced writers—but they are used with discretion. However, the inexperienced writer has a tendency to overuse the *weak* words (some students, for example, may use the word *interesting* five or six times in one paragraph) and to use carelessly the *overemphatic* words when the context calls for a more moderate synonym. If you have this problem, the clarity and style of your writing should improve if you make a determined effort to use more precise diction in your themes and reports.

EXERCISE 27

Rewrite the following sentences, substituting more precise words and phrases for the weak and overemphatic ones that are italicized.

1. We had a *fine* time on our vacation.

   _____

2. The man who sang the lead role had a *wonderful* voice.

   _____

3. The students had a *swell* time on their trip to New York.

   _____

4. Jones did a *terrific* job in organizing the committee on standards.

   _____

5. Gibson had a *good* reason for being late.

   _____

6. Senator Harris developed an *awful* headache; therefore, he was not able to fulfill the speaking engagement.

   _____

   _____

7. The movie had an *interesting* plot.

   _____

8. The City Council submitted a *fabulous* plan to construct a garbage disposal facility.

   _____

   _____

9. The football coach drew up a *tremendous* plan for enlarging the dressing rooms.

   _____

10. The entertainment committee announced to the student body their *amazing* plans for the senior dance.

    _____

_____

_____

11. Last night we had a *bad* storm that did much damage to the tobacco crop.

_____

_____

12. It was such a *lovely* day that the commander of the squadron ordered the pilots to fly a routine mission.

_____

_____

13. Helen has a *very nice* personality.

_____

14. Because it was a *beautiful* day, we decided to go fishing.

_____

15. The President gave an *interesting* speech on the dangers of inflation.

_____

EXERCISE 28

Rewrite the following sentences, substituting more precise words and phrases for the weak and overemphatic ones that are italicized.

1. An aspiring actor could gain *wonderful* experience by participating in amateur theatricals.

   _____

   _____

2. The author did a *very good* job in explaining his point of view.

   _____

3. We found the museum to be *very interesting*.

   _____

4. Most of the people we met seemed to be *very nice*.

   _____

5. Many *things* can be gained from television.

   _____

6. Television may prove to be a *good* medium of adult education.

   _____

7. The Governor gave a *splendid* speech when he dedicated the new state office building.

   _____

   _____

8. Ralph had a *tremendous* idea for improving the design of the boat.

   _____

9. The Chief of Police did his best to remedy the *bad* situation in the slum area of the city.

   _____

   _____

10. Mr. Woods has a *fabulous* personality.

    _____

11. Since it was a *beautiful* day, we decided to go on a picnic.

_____

12. He told me many *things* about farming that have been a great help to me.

_____

13. His dramatic way of teaching was *very interesting.*

_____

14. Mr. Roman has a *good* sense of humor.

_____

15. The networks did a *magnificent* job in covering the political convention.

_____

EXERCISE 29

Rewrite the following sentences, substituting more precise words and phrases for the weak and overemphatic ones that are italicized.

1. Most of the students found the class *interesting*.

   _____

2. The Urban Renewal Committee made a *tremendous* contribution to the welfare of the city.

   _____

   _____

3. The thought of being sent to Vietnam had a *bad* effect on the morale of the recruits.

   _____

   _____

4. The newly elected mayor seems to be a *very nice* fellow.

   _____

5. At the beginning of the second half he seemed to be *very tired*.

   _____

6. In my opinion his teaching methods were *very good*.

   _____

7. Sally said she had an *awful* time at the party.

   _____

8. *Ben Hur* was one of the most *interesting* movies I have ever seen.

   _____

9. We had a *very pretty* view from the window of our seaside hotel.

   _____

10. The electronics manufacturing plant in our city has announced some *terrific* plans for expansion.

    _____

    _____

11. The movie had a *very interesting* plot.

_____

12. The increase in crime in our city during the past ten years has been *amazing.*

_____

13. Joan has a *wonderful* voice.

_____

14. Senator Flanagan gave a *very good* speech when he visited our school.

_____

15. The *thing* that irritated me was the way he tried to impress the teacher.

_____

EXERCISE 30

Rewrite the following sentences, substituting more precise words and phrases for the weak and overemphatic ones that are italicized.

1. We really had a *nice* time on our tour of the French Quarter in New Orleans.

   _____

2. It is *amazing* that New Orleans is the second largest port in the country insofar as tonnage handled.

   _____

   _____

3. The first evening in New Orleans we had a *fine* dinner at the Oyster House, one of the most *interesting* restaurants I have ever seen.

   _____

   _____

4. After dinner, we went to one of the famous night clubs, where we saw a *terrific* floor show.

   _____

   _____

5. One of the *things* that impressed me most about New Orleans was the statue of Andrew Jackson in the middle of the square that bears his name.

   _____

   _____

6. The weather was *wonderful* during the first three days of our visit, but the day before we left, it rained and the temperature fell twenty degrees.

   _____

   _____

7. The first day in the Crescent City, we took a *grand* tour that introduced us to many of the *beautiful* sights in New Orleans.

   _____

   _____

8. During the day *a tremendous number* of people walk up and down Canal Street, where many of the shops and department stores are located.

_____

_____

9. Our guide was really a *swell* fellow, and he was a wellspring of *interesting* information.

_____

_____

10. Although we could not afford to buy any of them, we enjoyed looking at the *magnificent* antiques in the shops on Royal Street.

_____

_____

11. Many of the *fabulous* homes were built when New Orleans was ruled by France and Spain.

_____

_____

12. On our visit to the *ancient* St. Louis Cathedral, we enjoyed looking at the *pretty* pictures on display across the street from the church.

_____

_____

13. The *lovely* trees and shrubs that line the grass divide on Canal Street give the wide avenue its distinctive character.

_____

_____

14. The *thing* that impressed me most about New Orleans was the contrast between the old and the new.

_____

_____

15. The only *bad* memory I have of New Orleans is the afternoon we went to the races and I didn't cash a ticket.

_____

_____

Clichés

Competent writers usually make a determined effort to delete clichés from their formal writing, while many inexperienced writers use shopworn and trite expressions indiscriminately, often without even realizing they are using them. Precisely what does this term mean? The word *cliché* comes from the French verb *clicher*, meaning to stereotype. Thus, a cliché is an overworked, hackneyed expression that has become threadbare through excessive use, such as the following familiar expressions.

abreast of the times	method in his madness	center of attraction
all work and no play	sadder but wiser	few and far between
as luck would have it	too funny for words	time marches on
better late than never	sly as a fox	cool as a cucumber
by leaps and bounds	rotten to the core	pretty as a picture
easier said than done	commune with nature	sober as a judge
exception that proves the rule	bull in a china shop	darkness overtook us

Why should you eliminate clichés from your theme or report? Perhaps the most important reason is that a composition littered with clichés suggests that the writer has not thought deeply or creatively about his subject. Also, there is a chance that their meaning might not be clear to the reader. A cliché is in one sense like slang. Some clichés that are readily understood by one generation are foreign to another, although a large number of stock expressions persist, similar to those we have listed. Others slowly fade. For example, if an older writer used *trip the light fantastic* the teen-age reader would probably not have the foggiest idea what he was talking about, but the teen-ager's parents would immediately associate *trip the light fantastic* with dancing. This usage, of course, also works in the opposite way. The college freshman may use jargon that is readily understood by his age group but that baffles his teacher. For these reasons, clichés and slang expressions should be scarce in formal expository writing.

In proofreading your theme, one way to decide whether a doubtful expression is a cliché is to read the first part; then close your eyes and see if the last part automatically comes to mind. For example, *all work and . . . , as luck would . . . , better late than . . . , cool as a . . . ,* etc. Incidentally, you can more easily spot clichés and other flaws in your writing if you concentrate on one line at a time by using a ruler or a blank piece of paper or if you read the material aloud.

After you have found an obvious cliché in your writing, what is the next step? Let us try to look at the matter realistically. In the first place, all of us use clichés in ordinary speech, for they are part of the colloquial language that is embedded in our speech patterns. Therefore, it is not surprising that we use stock expressions in our writing, for writing in a sense is speech put down on paper. Even the professional writer will use a cliché now and then for the very good reason that he cannot think of anything better.

Following the same logic, the student writer is justified in using a cliché—as a matter of fact he is probably wise to do so—if he cannot think of a phrase that is as clear and expressive as the platitude. Consider this example:

> Last weekend I attended our national convention in Chicago. After checking into my hotel, I decided to take a stroll along State Street to enjoy the hubbub of the noontime rush. To my great astonishment I ran smack into my cousin—also from Birmingham—who was in Chicago on a business trip. Indeed, it is a small world.

The writer probably realized that *it is a small world* is a cliché. Yet this proverb says what he means and is probably clear to the average reader. In such an instance the writer is justified in using a cliché if he cannot think of an original phrase that is as vivid and clear as the common expression.

Thus the trained as well as the inexperienced writer will use a cliché now and then. However, the inept writer often uses clichés indiscriminately—mainly because the use of them saves him the trouble of thinking creatively about his subject. If you are guilty of this practice, you should look for clichés and get rid of them by substituting less routine language, as we have done in the following examples:

> Poor   Dr. Hart reads the daily newspaper and several weekly and monthly magazines *to stay abreast of the times.*
> Better Dr. Hart reads the daily newspaper and several weekly and monthly magazines *to keep well informed.*

Poor	The delegates at the convention *agreed to disagree.*
Better	The delegates at the convention *agreed to debate the issues.*

Poor	*As luck would have it,* Tom spotted his shipmate as he strolled through Central Park.
Better	*Luckily,* Tom spotted his shipmate as he strolled through Central Park.

Poor	Although he was not a brilliant student in college, Jack rose *by leaps and bounds* to one of the top executive positions in the company.
Better	Although he was not a brilliant student in college, Jack rose *rapidly* to one of the top executive positions in the company.

Poor	Pete almost reached the *depths of despair* before he finally made a sale.
Better	Pete had just about *given up all hope* before he finally made a sale.

Poor	The speech that Dr. Jordan gave at the graduation exercise *did justice to the occasion.*
Better	The speech that Dr. Jordan gave at the graduation exercise *was indeed appropriate.*

Poor	The aspiring writer who expects quick success is usually *doomed to disappointment.*
Better	The aspiring writer who expects quick success is usually *disappointed.*

Poor	Bowling a 600 series is *easier said than done.*
Better	Bowling a 600 series is *quite difficult* for most people.

Poor	Although Bill did not *feel equal to the occasion,* he gave an excellent speech at the football banquet.
Better	Although Bill had *serious misgivings about his oratorical ability,* he gave an excellent speech at the football banquet.

The intelligent reader will probably prefer the *better* example in every instance, for the diction is more original and mature. Thus if a composition is littered with clichés, the critical reader may judge the student to be untrained or incompetent. The use of clichés by professional writers as a technique to delineate character, having the person think and speak in clichés, is further proof of this point. The author of a short story, for example, will have one of his characters use clichés in his speech.

> The main reason I watch the news programs on television is to keep abreast of the times. But I also enjoy watching the sport programs, for all work and no play makes Jack a dull boy. The other night, as luck would have it, I saw a terrific murder mystery on the late show in which the private eye was cool as a cucumber. Of course, I don't spend all my time watching television. On Sunday afternoon, if the weather is nice, I take a walk through the park and commune with nature.

The fiction writer is saying in effect that the character in his story is a commonplace person who has little originality or imagination; his inane ideas expressed in stereotyped language prove this fact. The student writer whose theme is littered with clichés invites a similar judgment. Thus he should make a special effort to rid his theme of clichés by using more original language.

EXERCISE 31

The italicized words are clichés that detract from the force and originality of the writing. In the space following the sentences, substitute more original language for these italicized words.

1. What a miserably hot day! *You can say that again.*

   _____

2. The two teams *fought tooth and nail* until the horn sounded ending the game.

   _____

   _____

3. We did not expect Jerry to swallow the story *hook, line, and sinker.*

   _____

4. We did not get home from the dance until the *wee, small hours.*

   _____

5. Tim was full of *vim, vigor, and vitality.*

   _____

6. One should try to *hit a happy medium* in all that he does.

   _____

7. *As luck would have it,* the empty bottle kept him afloat.

   _____

8. After many *trials and tribulations,* we arrived in Florida for our spring vacation.

   _____

9. Good jobs nowadays are *few and far between.*

   _____

10. That is not the correct answer, but you are *on the right track.*

    _____

11. Swimming and fishing was *the order of the day.*

    _____

12. His chance to win the race seems slight. But *if there's a will, there's a way.*

_____

13. In atomic research we are determined *to be second to none.*

_____

14. The costume that she wore was *too beautiful for words.*

_____

15. I try *to keep abreast of the times* by reading several weekly magazines.

_____

EXERCISE 32

The italicized words are clichés that detract from the force and originality of the writing. In the space following the sentences, substitute more original language for these italicized words.

1. To pass the English course I had *to burn the midnight oil.*

   _____

2. He *showed his true colors* when his team lost the final game in the tournament.

   _____

3. *Last but not least,* I would like to discuss the role of sports in college.

   _____

4. *History tells us* that economics is one of the main causes of war.

   _____

5. He was *dead tired* after his long walk in the woods.

   _____

6. The new Benny Goodman album is *out of this world.*

   _____

7. We arose *at the crack of dawn* to pack our gear for the long hike.

   _____

8. On the football field Tom is perfectly coordinated, but on the dance floor he is *a bull in a china shop.*

   _____

   _____

9. The tickets to the dance are *selling like hot cakes.*

   _____

10. I decided to take a stroll through the park and *commune with nature.*

    _____

11. Jake was *brown as a berry* from his vacation in Florida.

    _____

12. The prosecuting attorney was *sly as a fox* in refuting the alibi of the defendant.

_____

13. From your description of the trip, I believe you are a *poet at heart.*

_____

14. *With animal cunning,* the prisoner evaded the police and escaped into Mexico.

_____

15. The city administration was *rotten to the core.*

_____

EXERCISE 33

The italicized words are clichés that detract from the force and originality of the writing. In the space following the sentences, substitute more original language for these italicized words.

1. Often *members of the fair sex* are not given equal consideration when it comes to promotions.

   _____

2. The action in the final game of the tournament was *fast and furious.*

   _____

3. During the depression in the 1930's jobs were *as scarce as hen's teeth.*

   _____

4. *It goes without saying* that Allan is a sharp businessman.

   _____

5. When he started to college, he was *as green as grass.*

   _____

6. After he cashed his first pay check, he stopped by the restaurant and ate hamburgers *to his heart's content.*

   _____

7. I joined the *motley crew* that gathered in front of the fraternity house.

   _____

8. Our mayor, John Brown, is *as honest as the day is long.*

   _____

9. The order of the sergeant to police the grounds was *no sooner said than done.*

   _____

10. We decided to drop by the restaurant after the game and *partake of refreshments.*

    _____

11. Unfortunately our plot to oust the chairman was *nipped in the bud.*

    _____

12. We decided to drop by the Student Union Building and *trip the light fantastic.*

_____

13. *Last but not least,* one must consider the sonnets of Shakespeare as a major contribution to world literature.

_____

14. *It stands to reason* that students need regular exercise.

_____

15. Tony worked in the field all day with only a short break for lunch. Obviously he has an *iron constitution.*

_____

EXERCISE 34

The italicized words are clichés that detract from the force and originality of the writing. In the space following the sentences, substitute more original language for these italicized words.

1. First I must check with the *powers that be* to see if I can get off Saturday.

   _____

2. The team was given a *royal reception* after they returned from Kansas City.

   _____

3. After his two week vacation in Las Vegas, he returned *sadder but wiser* to his job in Chicago.

   _____

4. We had time only to *scratch the surface* of this complex problem.

   _____

5. He finally faced one of the *stern realities* of life: he would have to get a job.

   _____

6. "All right," the coach told the team, "I am going to tell you *straight from the shoulder.*"

   _____

7. He earned enough money by the *sweat of his brow* to return to school for another year.

   _____

8. In *this day and age* one has a hard time making *the two ends meet.*

   _____

9. The movie was really *too funny for words.*

   _____

10. Douglas was a *tower of strength* to the other members of the team.

    _____

11. Both of us were able to swim to the shore before our boat sank to its *watery grave.*

    _____

12. The food served in the cafeteria *leaves a great deal to be desired.*

_____

13. Don't worry about his remark. Remember that *ignorance is bliss.*

_____

14. He seems *none the worse for wear* after his six months in the Army.

_____

15. When his teacher told him the Dean wanted to see him, he turned *white as a sheet.*

_____

9

Sentence Structure:

The Sentence Fragment, the Run-Together Sentence, and the Comma Splice

The sentence fragment, the run-together sentence, and the comma splice are three of the most common errors in sentence structure. They are serious mistakes because they detract from the clarity of a composition, branding the writer as untrained or careless. Be wise. Learn the fundamentals of sentence structure and avoid the mistakes that can be so damaging to an otherwise acceptable theme or report.

The Sentence Fragment

The sentence fragment or incomplete sentence or broken sentence (in our discussion and in the drills that follow we shall use the first term) is a word or group of words that lacks some feature of the conventional sentence pattern. The unintentional sentence fragment is a serious mistake, for it indicates the writer's failure to relate his ideas in a logical way, thus blurring his meaning.

Perhaps the best way to avoid this error is to know the essential qualities of a complete sentence. It is difficult to give a brief definition that will cover all forms of writing and speaking. Hence our definition is meant to be limited, relating to the type of composition you will ordinarily write in college and in your correspondence and reports after college.

A sentence is a unit of expression that is functionally and grammatically complete. It should have at least one main clause that has a subject (the part about which something is said) and the predicate (the part that says something about the subject). It is possible that the subject and/or predicate may be implied, especially in writing answers to direct questions. But such condensed sentences rarely appear in sound exposition and should be used with caution. The more desirable practice is to use the usual sentence patterns learned in previous composition courses.

USUAL PATTERNS

Declarative (makes a statement)	The opening-day game between the Reds and the Mets was postponed because of rain.
Imperative (gives a command)	Please close the door.
Interrogative (asks a question)	Are you going to the dance next Saturday?

UNCOMMON PATTERNS

Subject implied	Walk. (I walk to school.)
Predicate implied	John Ford. (John Ford is president of the senior class.)
Subject and predicate implied	Chicago. (I am going to Chicago.)

It follows, then, from what we have said that a fragment is a word or group of words punctuated as a complete sentence that is only part of a sentence. Although fragments appear in a variety of forms, the most common are separated dependent clauses and detached phrases of various kinds. They can usually be corrected by either joining them with a main clause or converting them into complete sentences.

Separated Dependent Clause

One of the most common fragments is the dependent clause punctuated as though it were a complete sentence. It is understandable how this mistake might come about, because a dependent clause resembles a sentence and, like a main clause, has a subject and predicate. Still the separated dependent clause is not grammatically complete, and it depends on a main clause for its full meaning. Its first word is usually a subordinate conjunction or a relative pronoun (see lists that follow). When you spot one of these words at the beginning of a would-be sentence, you should double check to make sure the unit is properly joined to a main clause.

SUBORDINATE CONJUNCTIONS

after	before	until
although	except	when
as	if	where
as if	since	whereas
as though	though	whether
because	unless	while

RELATIVE PRONOUNS

that	which	whom
what	who	whose
whatever	whoever	

Contains a Fragment (Wrong) We decided to drive to Chicago to see Notre Dame play Northwestern. Although the weatherman predicted snow and freezing temperatures.

Corrected We decided to drive to Chicago to see Notre Dame play Northwestern, although the weatherman predicted snow and freezing temperatures.

Comment Recalling the definition of a sentence, you can see that the first statement is grammatically as well as functionally complete; it has a subject and predicate and it can stand alone as expressing a complete thought. However, the last word group is not complete, because it depends upon the preceding main clause for its full meaning. Thus the last group of words in the incorrect example contains a fragment. You can avoid this sentence-structure error by joining the two clauses with a comma, as we did in the corrected example.

Contains a Fragment (Wrong) I shall always remember my teacher in business school. Who helped me to get a job with the government.

Corrected I shall always remember my teacher in business school, who helped me to get a job with the government.

Comment If you analyze the first clause in the wrong example, you will see that it has the components of a complete sentence, but the same cannot be said of the second clause, which is dependent on the main clause for its meaning. The grammatical function of the adjective clause is to describe *teacher*; therefore, it should be joined to the main clause, as in the corrected example.

Separated Phrases

In addition to separated dependent clauses, disjoined phrases are also frequently punctuated as complete sentences. We shall give examples of three different kinds of separated phrases: (1) the participial phrase, (2) the prepositional phrase, and (3) the explanatory phrase.

Contains a Fragment (Wrong)	Tom returned the wallet to the man and received a $10 reward. Proving that honesty is the best policy.
Corrected	(1) Tom returned the wallet to the man and received a $10 reward, proving that honesty is the best policy. (2) Tom returned the wallet to the man and received a $10 reward. His honesty did not go unrewarded.
Comment	Recalling the definition of a sentence, you will observe that the first part of the wrong example can stand by itself as a complete grammatical unit, but the second part cannot stand alone because it is a dependent phrase (having neither subject nor predicate). To remove the fragment the writer may either join the phrase to the main clause or convert it into a sentence as we have done in the corrected examples.
Contains a Fragment (Wrong)	Bob signed a contract to play professional baseball in one of the minor leagues. Without realizing that this move would prevent him from playing basketball in college.
Corrected	(1) Bob signed a contract to play professional baseball in one of the minor leagues without realizing that this move would prevent him from playing basketball in college.
Comment	If you know the basic requirements of a sentence, you will see that the first group of words in the wrong example is a complete unit of expression; however, the second group is not a complete thought unit but is dependent on the preceding main clause for its full meaning. You can eliminate this fragment by joining it with the main clause or by making it a separate sentence as we have done in the corrected example.
Contains a Fragment (Wrong)	Some errors in writing are considered minor and some are deemed serious. For example, fragments and run-together sentences.
Corrected	(1) Some errors in writing are considered minor and some are deemed serious—for example, fragments and run-together sentences. (2) Some errors in writing are considered minor and some are deemed serious. Among the gross errors are fragments and run-together sentences.
Comment	In the wrong example, the first group of words satisfies the requirements of a sentence, but the second group is merely a phrase, lacking both subject and predicate. Therefore, it should not be punctuated as if it were a sentence. The phrase will have to be either joined to the main clause or converted into a sentence, as we have done in the corrected example.

Finding and correcting fragments, as you can see from the examples, depends upon your being able to recognize word groups that are complete sentences and those that are not. If this point in sentence structure is still vague, we suggest you go back and review the definition of a sentence before studying the other examples that follow.

Contains a Fragment (Wrong)	I told Ralph I was sorry that I could not attend the banquet. Because I had already made plans to visit some friends in St. Louis.
Corrected	I told Ralph I was sorry that I could not attend the banquet, because I had already made plans to visit some friends in St. Louis.
Comment	If you study the wrong example you will see that the second clause is dependent on the first. Although it has a subject and a predicate, the second clause begins with a subordinate conjunction. By integrating the dependent clause with the main clause, the writer removes the fragment.
Contains a Fragment (Wrong)	Although the extent of the damage will not be known until a more accurate survey is made. The hurricane hit New Orleans with the force of an atomic explosion.
Corrected	Although the extent of the damage will not be known until a more accurate survey is made, the hurricane hit New Orleans with the force of an atomic explosion.
Comment	The difficulty in the wrong example is the same as in the previous one. Dependent clauses should not be punctuated as complete sentences; they should be joined to the main clause or reworded to form a complete sentence.
Contains a Fragment (Wrong)	There are definite reasons why we cannot expect a reduction in taxes this year. Such as the sending of our troops to Vietnam.
Corrected	There are definite reasons why we cannot expect a reduction in taxes this year, such as the sending of our troops to Vietnam.
Comment	A frequent cause of fragments is the writing of examples or illustrations as separate sentences. If the word group does not have the components of a standard sentence, it should be joined to the preceding sentence, as in the corrected example.
Contains a Fragment (Wrong)	There are a number of reasons why the prospects for world peace are worse now than a decade ago. For example, the loss in prestige of the UNO and the confused status of NATO.
Improved	There are a number of reasons why the prospects for world peace are worse now than a decade ago—for example, the loss in prestige of the UNO and the confused status of NATO.

Comment	The wrong example is comparable to the preceding one; the writer was probably tricked into thinking that an example can be punctuated as a sentence even though it does not have a subject and predicate.
Contains a Fragment (Wrong)	A number of causes of the riot have been suggested. The desire for better housing, equal educational opportunities, and freedom from discrimination in obtaining jobs.
Improved	A number of causes of the riot have been suggested: the desire for better housing, equal educational opportunities, and freedom from discrimination in obtaining jobs.
Improved	A number of causes of the riot have been suggested. Some of the factors mentioned were the desire for better housing, the need for equal educational opportunities, and the dissatisfaction with job discrimination.
Comment	In the first corrected example the writer has placed a colon at the end of the main clause, which indicates that a listing is to follow. If a colon is used in this way, it does not have to be followed by a complete sentence; however, the first letter of the first word of the listing should not be capitalized. In the second corrected example, the writer has made the listing of factors a complete sentence, in this way removing the fragment.
Contains a Fragment (Wrong)	Many of the graduate students bore a grudge against the Dean for one reason mainly. The fact that Clark received preference over the other candidates who applied for the fellowship.
Improved	Many of the graduate students bore a grudge against the Dean, because he gave Clark preference over the other candidates who applied for the fellowship.
Improved	Many of the graduate students bore a grudge against the Dean for one reason mainly. He gave Clark preferential treatment over the other candidates who applied for the fellowship.
Comment	Usually it is possible to combine the fragment with the preceding clause, but sometimes it is better to convert the fragment into a separate sentence.
Contains a Fragment (Wrong)	Our history teacher seemed to be dissatisfied with the performance of the class. So after the mid-term exams he announced his new policy. Giving more objective tests as a means of motivating students to read assignments carefully.
Improved	Our history teacher seemed to be dissatisfied with the performance of the class. So after the mid-term exams he announced his new policy, giving more objective tests as a means of motivating students to read assignments carefully.

Improved	Our history teacher seemed to be dissatisfied with the performance of the class. So after the mid-term exams he told us that he was going to give more objective tests as a means of motivating students to read assignments carefully.
Comment	In the first corrected example the writer removed the fragment by adding the verbal to the second main clause. In the second corrected example the writer integrated the fragment in a like manner, converting the verbal to an independent clause.

Run-Together Sentence and Comma Splice

Another common but serious mistake that recurs in student writing stems from the improper punctuation of independent clauses in compound sentences. We have divided this error into two parts: (1) the run-together (or fused) sentence and (2) the comma splice (or comma fault).

You will recall the several different types of sentences: simple, compound, and complex. A run-together sentence results when the writer fails to insert the necessary punctuation—a period or comma or semicolon—between independent clauses. A comma splice results when the writer uses a comma rather than a period or semicolon between independent clauses that are *not* joined by a coordinate conjunction (*and, but, for, nor, or*). If you are to avoid these errors you need to know several basic rules that govern the punctuation of independent clauses; we shall try to avoid confusion by concentrating on the general rules and not stressing the exceptions.

When two or more independent clauses are combined in a compound sentence they must be correctly punctuated. If they are joined by a coordinate conjunction (*and, but, for, nor, or*), a comma should be placed before the conjunction.

> At the foot of the mountain we made camp for the night, and the next morning we began our laborious ascent to the peak.

If two independent clauses are joined by a transitional word other than a coordinate conjunction (such words as *so, yet, thus, hence, however, moreover, consequently, furthermore, nevertheless, otherwise,* etc.), the independent clauses should be separated by a semicolon. If no coordinate conjunction or other transitional word joins the two independent clauses, they must be written as separate sentences or separated by a semicolon.

> I intend to spend my Christmas vacation working on my term paper; otherwise, I may end up with a failing grade in the course.

Comment In the above example the writer correctly placed a semicolon after *paper,* because *otherwise* is an adverbial conjunction—rather than a coordinate conjunction. Also he placed a comma after *otherwise,* a favored practice among many trained writers. A comma, however, is not required after the shorter connectives, such as, *so, yet, thus,* and *hence.*

<table>
<tr><td></td><td>Perhaps it would be better to enroll at a university in my home state; the savings in tuition and transportation would be considerable.</td></tr>
<tr><td>Comment</td><td>If the second independent clause is not preceded by a coordinate conjunction (and, but, for, nor, or), a semicolon is required to punctuate the compound sentence correctly. In all the examples, we shall assume that the writer wants to combine his clauses in compound sentences rather than use simple statements. In the last example note the absence of any conjunction, in which case a semicolon is needed to separate the independent clauses.</td></tr>
</table>

Now that you are acquainted with the positive rules, let us see how these rules are violated.

<table>
<tr><td>Run-Together</td><td>We spent the entire afternoon working on our pass defense for our coach felt that Lincoln High would exploit this weakness if their backs could not penetrate our line.</td></tr>
<tr><td>Improved</td><td>We spent the entire afternoon working on our pass defense, for our coach felt that Lincoln High would exploit this weakness if their backs could not penetrate our line.</td></tr>
<tr><td>Comment</td><td>The writer needs a comma before for, because for is a coordinate conjunction that joins the two independent clauses.</td></tr>
<tr><td>Run-Together</td><td>The boat was almost filled with water and we had to race full speed for the shore.</td></tr>
<tr><td>Improved</td><td>The boat was almost filled with water, and we had to race full speed for the shore.</td></tr>
<tr><td>Comment</td><td>The mistake here is like the previous one. We have two independent clauses joined by and, a coordinate conjunction. Thus a comma is needed before and to avoid a run-together sentence.</td></tr>
<tr><td>Run-Together</td><td>Dr. Collier attended the medical convention in London afterwards he spent two weeks vacationing in France.</td></tr>
<tr><td>Improved</td><td>Dr. Collier attended the medical convention in London; afterwards, he spent two weeks vacationing in France.</td></tr>
<tr><td>Comment</td><td>In this example we have two independent clauses (or groups of words that can stand alone as complete thoughts) that are not joined by a coordinate conjunction (and, but, for, nor, or); therefore, they must be separated by a semicolon.</td></tr>
<tr><td>Run-Together</td><td>It is becoming increasingly difficult to obtain a good job without a college education therefore more and more students are entering the colleges and universities of the United States.</td></tr>
<tr><td>Improved</td><td>It is becoming increasingly difficult to obtain a good job without a college education; therefore, more and more students are entering the colleges and universities of the United States.</td></tr>
<tr><td>Comment</td><td>In this example we have two independent clauses. The second is introduced by therefore, an adverbial conjunction, which must be preceded by a semicolon. The comma that follows is optional, although most experienced writers would use it.</td></tr>
<tr><td>Run-Together</td><td>Generally Dr. Brewer's lectures are not too stimulating however now and then he gives one that is superb.</td></tr>
<tr><td>Improved</td><td>Generally Dr. Brewer's lectures are not too stimulating; however, now and then he gives one that is superb.</td></tr>
</table>

Comment	This example is similar to the previous one. In the first case the writer has a run-together sentence, for he does not properly separate his independent clauses with a semicolon. In the improved example he solves this problem by placing a semicolon before *however* and a comma after the introductory adverb.

If a writer incorrectly punctuates a sentence by using a comma rather than a semicolon or period, he commits the comma splice error. Again, as in the case of the run-together sentence, we are concerned with punctuating independent clauses, groups of words that can stand alone as complete thoughts. The positive rule has been previously stated: Independent clauses joined by coordinate conjunctions (*and, but, for, nor, or*) require a comma before the conjunction. Independent clauses joined by conjunctive adverbs (such as *however, moreover, nevertheless, therefore,* etc.) or independent clauses that have no conjunctions must be separated by a semicolon.

Comma Splice	The number of commercial airliners that have crashed in recent months is shocking, nowadays I am almost afraid to send a letter by air mail.
Improved	The number of commercial airliners that have crashed in recent months is shocking; nowadays I am almost afraid to send a letter by air mail.
Comment	In the original example the writer has committed a comma splice; he needs a semicolon rather than a comma between the independent clauses inasmuch as they are not joined by a coordinate conjunction.
Comma Splice	The number of holiday basketball tournaments is alarming, it is difficult to imagine when the players find time to catch up on their studies.
Improved	The number of holiday basketball tournaments is alarming, for it is difficult to imagine when the players find time to catch up on their studies.
Comment	The semicolon is a useful mark of punctuation—but it should not be overused. In the improved example the comma will suffice, because the writer has used the coordinate conjunction *for* to join the independent clauses.
Comma Splice	The large number of high school dropouts is indeed a problem that calls for serious study, a practical solution must be found to keep students in school.
Improved	The large number of high school dropouts is indeed a problem that calls for serious study; a practical solution must be found to keep students in school.
Comment	As in the previous example the writer has a comma splice because he failed to join or separate the independent clauses by using a semicolon or a coordinate conjunction.
Comma Splice	It is difficult to envision any real practical benefits—other than propaganda—that will result from a landing on the moon, some of the leading American scientists have, in fact, recommended radical reductions in Federal spending for this program.

Improved	It is difficult to envision any real practical benefits—other than propaganda—that will result from a landing on the moon; some of the leading American scientists have, in fact, recommended radical reductions in Federal spending for this program.
Comment	The comma splice resulted from the writer's failure to do one of two things: (1) to use a semicolon rather than a comma and (2) to use a coordinate conjunction after the comma. In the improved example the writer corrected the comma splice by using a semicolon.
Comma Splice	The pollution of our rivers and streams has been debated in the U.S. Congress and in the state legislatures, however, little has been done to solve this mammoth problem.
Improved	The pollution of our rivers and streams has been debated in the U.S. Congress and in the state legislatures; however, little has been done to solve this mammoth problem.
Comment	If the second independent clause is introduced by a conjunctive adverb (such as *however, moreover, consequently, nevertheless, therefore, furthermore,* etc.) a semicolon rather than a comma should be used to separate the clauses as the writer has done in the improved example.

The *fragment*, the *run-together* sentence, and the *comma splice*—as we said at the outset—are serious sentence structure errors that not only detract from the clarity of a theme or report but also suggest the writer's literary ignorance. They are considered gross errors in college composition and business correspondence; therefore, you would be wise to learn the correct structures so thoroughly that you could use them with little or no conscious thought.

EXERCISE 35

Read each statement carefully; then decide whether it is correct or contains an error in sentence structure. No statement contains more than one error. Indicate your decision by placing the appropriate symbol in the left-hand column next to the sentence.

C   *Correct*
Frag.   *Sentence Fragment*
R.T.   *Run-Together Sentence*
C.S.   *Comma Splice*

_____ 1. I like the way Mr. Clark taught his classes, he had no trouble holding the attention of the students.

_____ 2. I went to a private boarding school from the seventh grade through high school.

_____ 3. The idea of my parents having to appear in court for something I had done.

_____ 4. Building more and better bombers and keeping some airborne at all times.

_____ 5. When the car reached the intersection, the light turned yellow and the driver quickly slammed on his brakes.

_____ 6. Being admitted to a college becomes more difficult every year.

_____ 7. Speeding construction on foreign bases to deter aggression.

_____ 8. Sometimes Professor Green is not too cooperative but most of the time he goes out of his way to help his students.

_____ 9. Conservation of food, water, shelter, wildlife, and property of others.

_____ 10. I believe there is a kind fate that guides my destiny, the trip to St. Louis had a happy outcome after all.

_____ 11. Our offense clicked like a well-oiled machine our defense was the dread of opposing coaches.

_____ 12. Some of which may promote sound judgment.

_____ 13. Perhaps it would be best not to anticipate the future, there seems to be an irony in human affairs that prevents things from turning out the way one expects.

_____ 14. Why do some students wait so long to continue their education?

_____ 15. Thus trying to prove who has the best boat.

EXERCISE 36

Read each statement carefully; then decide whether it is correct or contains an error in sentence structure. No statement contains more than one error. Indicate your decision by placing the appropriate symbol in the left-hand column next to the sentence.

C   *Correct*
Frag.   *Sentence Fragment*
R.T.   *Run-Together Sentence*
C.S.   *Comma Splice*

_____ 1. Sally was not certain if she would go home for the weekend, she was behind in her reading assignments and worried about the mid-term exams.

_____ 2. The growing congestion at metropolitan airports presents new problems every year perhaps the only solution may be a vast expansion and modernization of passenger trains that have become almost extinct.

_____ 3. Since most of the employees at the resort hotel were college students on their summer vacations.

_____ 4. I hope that you will do well in your studies and enjoy the companionship of your new friends.

_____ 5. The incredible growth of urban and suburban shopping centers and the effect they have had on downtown department stores.

_____ 6. Our coach spent the entire practice session reviewing the formations that Washington High, our next opponent, had used in their last game, he told us again and again that Washington would be hard to beat.

_____ 7. Although Hamlet had convincing evidence that his uncle had murdered his father.

_____ 8. The workers wanted an increase in hourly pay and definite assurance that automation would be curtailed but their demands were rejected by the company officials at the first round of the bargaining talks.

_____ 9. Perhaps the ultimate solution to the problems created by the nightmarish growth of metropolitan areas is a special tax deduction for those who live in small towns.

_____ 10. The Captain became angry when he found some old newspapers in the corner of the barracks, consequently our week-end liberty was cancelled.

_____ 11. Recent national statistics have confirmed a fact that most people already suspected a large percentage of teen-age marriages end in the divorce courts.

_____ 12. If I can force myself to save some money, I am going to take a trip to Spain next summer and visit my uncle.

_____ 13. I looked out the window of the airliner, to my surprise I could see nothing but water in all directions.

_____ 14. Besides the heroin smuggled into the country aboard ships and planes from Europe and the Near East.

_____ 15. I was tired of the humdrum monotony of life in a small town so I decided to move to Chicago.

Lesson 10

Sentence Structure:

Faulty Pronoun Reference

Faulty pronoun reference is another sentence-structure error that detracts from the clarity and precision of writing. Therefore, you should use pronouns with care, keeping in mind that a statement or question that is perfectly clear to you might be misleading to the reader.

The essential cause of faulty pronoun reference can be traced to the manner in which we think, that is, to the way the mind actually works. Much of our thinking is done in visual images that are captioned by pronouns rather than specific nouns. For example, a sailor walking through Times Square in New York may reflect, "I haven't heard from him for a long time." Simultaneously a picture of *him* (a former shipmate now stationed in Norfolk) comes to his mind. The same process undoubtedly takes place when we write; that is, when we use a pronoun, a more or less specific image comes to our minds. However, we cannot be at all sure that a similar phenomenon will take place in the mind of the reader unless our pronouns clearly refer to aforementioned words. The grammatical term *antecedent* designates the word for which the pronoun stands.

In order to explain this error more clearly, we have divided faulty pronoun reference into three types: (1) *divided reference,* (2) *implied reference,* and (3) *broad reference.* The best way to understand these terms is to study concrete examples, noting how the faulty reference is an obstacle to clear understanding and how the error may be corrected by rewriting the sentence or merely by supplying a specific reference word.

Divided Pronoun Reference

Divided pronoun reference is also termed *ambiguous* reference, for the vague pronoun can refer to more than one person, as in the following example:

Divided Reference   Mary told her sister that her car had been stolen.

Immediately the reader wonders, "Whose car was stolen? Did the car belong to Mary or did it belong to her sister?" Such a misuse of pronouns can make a statement in your theme baffling to the reader. Moreover, such a slip-up in business correspondence or in a legal document might cost the individual or his company a considerable sum or embarrassment and trouble. The examples and comments that follow demonstrate the need for careful pronoun reference. For if your reference is not clear, the reader has to guess what you are trying to say, and he may guess incorrectly.

Divided Reference	The members of the Senate tried in vain to convince the general public that they should assume the responsibility rather than the President of the United States.
Improved	The members of the Senate tried in vain to convince the general public that the people, rather than the President, should assume the responsibility for improving the schools.
Comment	In the divided example it is not clear who should assume the responsibility: the members of the Senate or the general public. To solve the problem no special rules need to be applied, except to ask yourself this practical question. How can I rewrite the vague statement so the meaning will be perfectly clear to the reader?
Divided Reference	Professor Desmond told David that his letter to the editor would be published in the school newspaper.
Improved	Professor Desmond told David that his (David's) letter to the editor would be published in the school newspaper.
Comment	The improved example may be a little awkward, but the meaning is clear, whereas the meaning in the divided example is ambiguous. Sometimes the preceding sentence will clarify the pronoun reference, but it is a risky business to leave too much to the imagination of the reader. Where clarity is involved, it is better to be too obvious than too subtle.
Divided Reference	Tom's brother told him that his notice from the draft board had come in the morning mail.

Improved	Tom's brother told him, "Tom, your notice from the draft board came in the morning mail."
Comment	Sometimes the use of dialogue is the best way to clarify divided pronoun reference, as seems to be true in this case.
Divided Reference	The sergeant told the corporal that his orders had finally been received, transferring him to Germany.
Improved	The sergeant broke the sad news to his assistant. "Corporal, I just received orders transferring you to Germany."
Comment	This example, of course, is comparable to the previous one. In the improved example, there is no doubt who is being transferred to Germany—just as there should be no possible doubt when you use a pronoun to refer to a preceding person, place, or thing.

Implied Pronoun Reference

Implied pronoun reference is a recurring problem in scholastic and professional writing, for the imprecise use of pronouns is common in speaking and informal composition. This ingrained language pattern is bound to assert a strong influence on our writing style no matter what the occasion might be. But there are differences between ordinary speech and standard expository writing, one being the fact that formal writing should be more precise. Thus *implied pronoun reference* that is acceptable in speech may be considered wrong in a theme or report, although it follows that a person's speech (as well as his writing) should improve if he tries to make his pronoun reference clear. Consider this statement:

Implied Reference	They make many poor movies in Hollywood.

The pronoun *they* is vague, for *they* implies a number of possibilities: the producers, the directors, the actors, etc. As in divided reference, the reader is forced to guess what the writer means. In more formal writing the reader should not have to guess; the writer should express his thoughts in precise and unequivocal terms. Eliminating *implied pronoun reference* from your themes and reports will help you to acquire this necessary precision.

If you detect *implied pronoun reference* in your theme or report, all you have to do is remove the pronoun and substitute a specific word or phrase. In other words, you should clearly state what is implied.

Implied Reference	While traveling through Oklahoma, we visited an Indian reservation and discovered that they were like ordinary Americans in most respects.
Improved	While traveling through Oklahoma, we visited an Indian reservation and discovered that the Cherokee Indians were like ordinary Americans in most respects.
Comment	The meaning of the improved example as compared with the poor example is much clearer; the reader does not have to stop and try to figure out what the writer means by *they*.

Implied Reference	Although the Communists have taken over in Poland, they are fighting to regain their basic freedoms.
Improved	Although the Communists have taken over in Poland, the citizens are fighting to regain their basic freedoms.
Comment	In studying this example, you might be well advised to recall the standard definition of a pronoun. "A pronoun is a word that takes the place of a noun or another pronoun." If you cannot clearly relate the pronoun to a specific antecedent, the chances are you have committed the error of implied pronoun reference.
Implied Reference	A food shortage developed, and they had to import food to keep the people from starving.
Improved	A food shortage developed, and the government officials had to import food to keep the people from starving.
Comment	The problem was solved in the improved example by substituting a noun for the pronoun. If you make a definite effort to follow this principle in your writing, your themes and reports are almost bound to improve in clarity and precision.

Broad Pronoun Reference

The problem of *broad pronoun reference* is similar to that of *implied reference,* for the antecedent of the pronoun is implied rather than clearly expressed. But an important distinction should be made. In implied reference no antecedent whatever is expressed, while in broad reference the antecedent is a broad idea or concept rather than a specific noun or verbal. In either case the reader is asked to do the writer's work, namely, to discover a relationship between a pronoun and an implied noun or between the pronoun and a broad idea.

You can easily solve the problem of broad pronoun reference when writing or proofreading your theme if you will recall the definition of a pronoun: "A pronoun is a word that takes the place of a noun or another pronoun." Then when you use a pronoun double check to make certain that the antecedent is clear. If the pronoun does not refer to a specific word but to a general statement, you probably have broad pronoun reference, as in the following example:

Broad Reference	Working during the day and going to school at night are difficult for most students, but *this* strengthens the will and often leads to outstanding success in later life.

Precisely what does the writer mean by *this* in the above sentence? The term *broad reference* is fitting, because the meaning of *this* covers a broad range of possibilities. Does the reader mean *this determination* or *this type of schedule* or *this handicap?* The reader must supply the answer; often, though, he will not go to the trouble of trying to understand. Or he may try but fail to guess the intended meaning. Hence the conscientious writer will take pains to make his pronoun reference clear.

Broad Reference	Hamlet hid from the present, ignored the future, and took refuge in the past. He demonstrated this during the first two acts of the play.
Improved	Hamlet hid from the present, ignored the future, and took refuge in the past. He showed this tendency to procrastinate during the first two acts of the play.
Improved	Hamlet hid from the present, ignored the future, and took refuge in the past. He pursued these evasions during the first two acts of the play.
Comment	In the first improved example the writer solved the reference problem by having *this* modify a definite noun phrase *tendency to procrastinate*, a phrase that implies the three actions in the first sentence. In the second improved example the writer uses a plural construction *these evasions*, the noun being a general synonym for the three actions in the first sentence.
Broad Reference	Some of the classes were combined and met in the same room. This irritated the faculty, but as always the Dean got his way.
Improved	Some of the classes were combined and met in the same room. This arrangement irritated the faculty, but as always the Dean got his way.
Comment	Broad reference can easily lead to a misunderstanding by the reader. It is an easy matter to place a specific noun after the pronoun, as we did in the improved example. Such a change usually makes the sentence clearer.
Broad Reference	Grain was blown from the soil, and livestock perished from lack of water and pasture. This was the final blow for many of the distressed farmers.
Improved	Grain was blown from the soil, and livestock perished from lack of water and pasture. This prolonged drought was the final blow for many of the distressed farmers.
Comment	In the improved example the reader is given the specific cause of the distress. In the poor example the reader may be somewhat confused, wondering if *this* refers to the soil problem or the livestock problem.
Broad Reference	Entering the subway, I turned to the right rather than to the left and caught the wrong train. This would not have happened if I had been paying closer attention to the signs.
Improved	Entering the subway, I turned to the right rather than to the left and caught the wrong train. This mistake would not have happened if I had been paying closer attention to the signs.
Comment	As in the previous example, the writer has used *this* in a broad sense to suggest both *turning* and *catching*. The reader may have to pause several seconds to puzzle out the reference, but he does not have to hesitate when reading the improved version.
Broad Reference	When the United States government unloads its surpluses on the international market, it hurts the economies of other countries that we are trying to help.

Improved	The unloading of surpluses on the international market by the United States Government may hurt the countries we are trying to help.
Comment	In the poor example the pronoun *it* apparently refers to the broad idea expressed by the dependent clause. Perhaps the best way to solve the problem of broad reference is to get rid of the pronoun altogether—as the writer has done in the improved example—making the sentence not only clearer but also easier to read.

In the section on *inflated diction,* we advised you to make your writing conform more to your speech patterns as a way to avoid flowery or pretentious language; however, we qualified our statement by listing certain differences between writing and speech. Another difference you can add to the list relates to the use of pronouns. When we speak, most of us use pronouns rather loosely and carelessly; understandably this habit often carries over to writing, causing vagueness or ambiguity. If you will remember that a pronoun is a word that takes the place of a noun or another pronoun and try to make your pronouns refer to specific antecedents, your writing will be clearer and you will have a better chance to win the reader to your point of view.

EXERCISE 37

Read each statement carefully; then decide whether it is correct or contains an error in sentence structure. No statement contains more than one error. Indicate your decision by placing the appropriate symbol in the left-hand column next to the statement.

C   Correct
Frag.   Sentence Fragment
R.T.   Run-Together Sentence
C.S.   Comma Splice
F.R.   Faulty Pronoun Reference

_____   1. Although each of the encyclopedias I examined had its merits and limitations.

_____   2. All planes were grounded because of the severe snow storm hence I had to take a train to Washington and stay overnight at a hotel.

_____   3. Juvenile delinquency may seem remote, but they constitute a fairly large percentage of the youth in most cities and towns.

_____   4. When I received the notification to report to the induction center for my physical examination.

_____   5. Some composition students strain to achieve a literary effect and produce a brand of writing that is ridiculous.

_____   6. The highway is narrow and curvy and hilly, consequently I left home early to allow myself plenty of time to make the trip.

_____   7. Since I wasted much of my time in high school worrying about sports and figuring out schemes to do as little work as possible.

_____   8. When you are assigned a topic for your reference paper, you should go to the library at your first opportunity; they have reference books on almost every subject imaginable.

_____   9. Many careless mistakes could be found if the student would proofread his theme aloud.

_____   10. Our boat was seaworthy and could stand the buffeting of the waves but we were afraid to make the voyage to Trinidad without an experienced navigator.

_____ 11. Our football team must win its game this afternoon against Southern, otherwise we have no chance to receive an invitation to the Sugar Bowl.

_____ 12. Mr. Cox is an experienced corporation lawyer who is also active in civic affairs. This should make him an outstanding candidate for mayor in the primary election.

_____ 13. Serving a hitch in one of the branches of the armed forces develops self-reliance. Self-reliance in looking after one's own interests.

_____ 14. Many students seem to have a fear of writing but appear to have a capacity for expressing their thoughts clearly in conversation.

_____ 15. Mr. Ewing is presently a member of the school board and serves on the Mayor's Advisory Committee. This proves that he has a lively interest in community affairs.

EXERCISE 38

Read each statement carefully; then decide whether it is correct or contains an error in sentence structure. No statement contains more than one error. Indicate your decision by placing the appropriate symbol in the left-hand column next to the statement.

C   Correct
Frag.   Sentence Fragment
R.T.   Run-Together Sentence
C.S.   Comma Splice
F.R.   Faulty Pronoun Reference

_____ 1. He now holds a high position in the school district and is highly respected in the community. This is proof that others saw his abilities as I did.

_____ 2. I could not return to my bunk so I decided to stay up and drink coffee and smoke my pipe.

_____ 3. Many students believe there is a vast difference between writing and speaking.

_____ 4. A chapter from the productive life of a man who was blind from birth.

_____ 5. We have had disagreements with our playmates, and in most instances they were soon forgotten.

_____ 6. The traffic is usually heavy, therefore, I allow myself ample time to get to work.

_____ 7. Since he acquired certain insights into the realities of politics.

_____ 8. One of the most significant American space achievements took place August 12, 1960, when they launched the Echo I balloon.

_____ 9. The destroyer was an old rust bucket but to her crew she was the best ship in the fleet.

_____ 10. The experience made me appreciate more than ever the important job the elementary and high school teachers are doing.

_____ 11. The eleven months that followed were filled with happiness and hope. Hope that we would always be together.

_____ 12. He is well versed in many subjects and is an articulate speaker. This helps to make him an excellent teacher.

_____ 13. In the past I have greatly enjoyed watching television, however, now I will not have time to see many programs.

_____ 14. I was filled with the usual forebodings that precede most new undertakings.

_____ 15. Although it is the most complete book I have seen.

EXERCISE 39

Read each statement carefully; then decide whether it is correct or contains an error in sentence structure. No statement contains more than one error. Indicate your decision by placing the appropriate symbol in the left-hand column next to the statement.

C	*Correct*
Frag.	*Sentence Fragment*
R.T.	*Run-Together Sentence*
C.S.	*Comma Splice*
F.R.	*Faulty Pronoun Reference*

_____ 1. While in South Dakota, we stopped to visit in a small town and found they were host to a Shrine convention.

_____ 2. I certainly hope all of you are in reasonably good health and high spirits for the holiday season.

_____ 3. Making a quick turn from the alley, I ran into the back of a car that was parking on the left side of the street. This would not have happened if I had been concentrating on my driving.

_____ 4. The recruiting sergeant did not know how long I would stay at Fort Knox he could not say definitely when I would be eligible for promotion.

_____ 5. My teacher gave me the three required books of poetry to study for my division, he also told me all the rules and regulations.

_____ 6. None of which he had any proof or real reason to believe.

_____ 7. The employees want higher wages and more security, but this will probably not materialize because of the many unemployed people in the area.

_____ 8. Food products such as bread and bakery goods, beverages, and other items too numerous to mention.

_____ 9. I was not eighteen until August, therefore, I had to wait a few months before I went job hunting.

_____ 10. In some high schools they force the students to do their homework.

_____ 11. I glanced downward at the terrain and to my dismay there was nothing but rough and swampy ground.

_____ 12. Although the intrigue was devised by Iago to bring about the downfall of Othello.

_____ 13. I was bored with my dull home life, moreover I resented the restrictions placed on me by my parents.

_____ 14. My plans for the summer are rather vague at present, but I hope to take a trip to New York or San Francisco.

_____ 15. The individual members of the cast had the ability to convince the audience that they were part of the action.

EXERCISE 40

Read each statement carefully; then decide whether it is correct or contains an error in sentence structure. No statement contains more than one error. Indicate your decision by placing the appropriate symbol in the left-hand column next to the statement.

C   *Correct*
Frag.   *Sentence Fragment*
R.T.   *Run-Together Sentence*
C.S.   *Comma Splice*
F.R.   *Faulty Pronoun Reference*

_____ 1. A talented writer has unlimited opportunities in Hollywood. They make movies on every theme imaginable.

_____ 2. Although a part-time job often doesn't take up as much of the student's time as social activities.

_____ 3. Typing outside assignments will be of great advantage to a student in college.

_____ 4. New York City is known as the entertainment capital of the world top-name performers from various countries congregate there.

_____ 5. Because it was right out of the manual and still fresh in my mind.

_____ 6. She favored me and gave me odd jobs to do because I was the youngest kid in the class. This gave me more confidence.

_____ 7. A grizzled old man stopped me and asked for some money to buy food.

_____ 8. One acre is devoted to a garden plot, the rest of the land is sown in small grain of some type.

_____ 9. As we walked toward Broadway, we could hear the horns from taxi cabs warning pedestrians that they had the right of way.

_____ 10. By noon the temperature was too high to work on the aircraft so we would return to our barracks or go to the canteen.

_____ 11. Riding herd on teen-agers is much more difficult than working in a coal mine.

_____ 12. I have a great desire to travel in foreign countries and become closely acquainted with the natives. From this I expect to acquire a liberal education.

_____ 13. The only difference being the effect it has on people.

_____ 14. Mr. Johnson would check our books and if they were not complete he would give us a failing grade.

_____ 15. Corn is now gathered and shucked by machine. They harvest the crops in a fraction of the time that was formerly required.

Lesson 11

Sentence Structure:
Faulty Parallelism

If a person lost a black, half-inch button off his coat he probably would not replace it with a red, two-inch button. His sense of proportion and harmony would tell him to use a button like the one he lost.

In like manner, parts of a sentence that have the same thought value or function should be in the same grammatical form. We discussed *parallelism* earlier in the section on outlining, saying that topics or subtopics of the outline similar in thought value should be expressed in similar language. For instance, in the topic outline for the theme "My Favorite Outdoor Sports," the main divisions were swimming, fishing, and hunting. The three sports are equal in thought and form. In this case we used a series of gerunds (verbal nouns): *swimming, fishing,* and *hunting.* It appears that the three sports are of equal importance, since they are expressed in parallel language. But if the series were expressed like this: "My favorite sports are swimming, to fish in rivers and lakes, and hunting," the reader might have to stop and ponder before he could be sure that the sports are of corresponding value. In a figurative sense the names of the sports are similar to the buttons on the coat. The sports have the same function (or thought value) and importance, so they should be expressed in the same grammatical form: swimming, fishing, and hunting.

As you can see, we are dealing basically with the question of coordination: sentence elements joined by coordinate conjunctions or other sentence elements of similar importance. To repeat, similar ideas within a sentence should be expressed in the same grammatical form. Now let us examine several of the common ways that the principle of *parallelism* is violated in writing, leading to the serious sentence-structure error termed *faulty parallelism*.

Two or more sentence elements that have the same function should be in the same grammatical form.

Poor	Baker was intelligent, determined, and had a dynamic personality.
Better	Baker was intelligent, determined, and dynamic.
Comment	*Intelligent* and *determined* in the preceding sentence describe Baker; both words are predicate adjectives. If the writer starts a series of predicate adjectives, he should not break the series by interjecting a verb, as he has done in the poor example. To do so is to commit faulty parallelism.
Poor	Through these organizations parents become acquainted with teachers and how their child is doing in school.
Better	Through these organizations parents *become* acquainted with teachers and *learn* how their children are doing in school.
Comment	The conjunction *and* should join like things: *bread* and *butter* (two nouns); *interesting* and *enjoyable* (two adjectives); *to fish* and *to hunt* (two infinitives). In the above sentence the writer should have a verb after *and* as well as before it.
Poor	Some predictable faults of the average individual are an irresponsible attitude, the inability to see one's own faults, and everyone being basically selfish.
Better	Some predictable faults of the average individual are an irresponsible *attitude,* the *inability* to see one's own faults, and a selfish *disposition* that is all too common.
Comment	In the poor example the writer started a series of noun objects; then all of a sudden he shifted to an indefinite pronoun, breaking his parallel pattern and creating an awkward effect.
Poor	I have been accused of being rough, hardheaded, and a determined individual.
Better	I have been accused of being rough, hardheaded, and determined.
Comment	Without going into a grammatical analysis of the poor example, the student can see that *rough* and *hardheaded* are in the same category but *determined individual* is different. The revised sentence has a better rhythm and the meaning is immediately clear.
Poor	A person may pursue his goal at college, at a trade school, a military career, or in industry.
Better	A person may pursue his goal at college, at a trade school, in the military service, or in industry.

Comment	Again without going into a complicated grammatical analysis, the student can see the element in the poor example that should be changed to make the sentence parallel.

When correlative conjunctions (that is, conjunctions used in pairs such as not only—but also; neither—nor; either—or) appear in a sentence, the same part of speech (noun, verb, adjective, etc.) should come after the second conjunction as after the first.

Poor	*Either* he is right *or* wrong.
Better	He is *either* right *or* wrong.
Comment	In the poor example a pronoun, *he*, follows the first conjunction, while an adjective, *wrong*, follows the second conjunction. In the corrected version both conjunctions are followed by adjectives.
Poor	*Neither* is John too proud *nor* too busy to do the job.
Better	John is *neither* too proud *nor* too busy to do the job.
Comment	In the poor example a verb, *is*, follows the first conjunction, while an adverb, *too*, follows the second one. In the corrected example both conjunctions are followed by adverbs.
Poor	*Not only* does he play a guitar *but also* he sings.
Better	He *not only* plays a guitar *but also* sings.
Comment	In the poor example the first conjunction is followed by a verb, *does*, while the second is followed by a pronoun, *he*, causing *faulty parallelism*.

Another sentence-structure problem that is closely akin to *faulty parallelism* (and shall be so designated in the exercises that follow the discussion) is the needless shift of *person, tense,* or *voice* within the sentence or paragraph.

Poor	I enjoy the Christmas holidays, for you have a chance to visit your friends and relatives.
Poor	The hunters spent the afternoon trudging through the woods and spend the evening relaxing before the log fire in their cabin.
Poor	We left Peoria about noon, and Chicago was reached in three hours.

In the first example the writer shifts *person*, in the second, *tense*, in the third, *voice*. Such needless shifts in a theme or report are awkward, detracting from the smooth flow of language. Moreover, the shifts in point of view within a sentence or paragraph may be a stumbling block to clear communication.

The point of view (person, tense, or voice) should be consistent within a sentence or paragraph.

SHIFT IN PERSON

Poor	One reason why I appreciate classical music is the enjoyment and relaxation you get from listening to it.
Better	I like classical music because it helps me to relax.
Comment	In the poor example the writer shifts from the first to the second person.

Poor	I still remember that the heat was so intense it felt as though you were standing over a fire.
Better	I recall that the heat was so intense it made me feel that I was standing over a fire.
Comment	In the poor example the writer also shifts from *I* to *you*—perhaps the most common shift found in student writing.

SHIFT IN TENSE

Poor	The first morning at camp we swam across the lake and lie on the sandy beach most of the afternoon.
Better	The first morning at camp we swam across the lake and lay on the sandy beach most of the afternoon.
Comment	In the poor example the student changed the tense of his verbs from the past to the present: *swam* to *lie*. A needless switch in the tense of the verb may be a problem in proofreading rather than logic, for in most instances there is no explainable reason why the writer should want to make such a change.
Poor	We parked our car at the harbor and rented one of the boats, which we use to get to Twelve Mile Island.
Better	We parked our car at the harbor and rented one of the boats, which we used to get to Twelve Mile Island.
Comment	The problem in the poor example should be obvious: A careless shift from the past to the present tense: from *parked* and *rented* to *use*.

SHIFT IN VOICE

Poor	With greater attention, the instructions could be understood, and we would not have to ask the professor to explain the lesson out of class.
Better	With greater attention, we could understand the instructions and not have to ask the professor to explain the lesson outside of class.
Comment	In the active voice the subject does the acting; in the passive voice the subject is acted upon. The poor example begins in the passive voice and abruptly shifts to the active. Such a shift may be avoided by placing the personal pronoun *we* near the beginning of the sentence.
Poor	The members of the fraternity decided to ask the Dean of Men for permission to hold their spring dance in a nearby city; thus certain problems, such as hotel accommodations for their dates, could be avoided.
Better	The members of the fraternity decided to ask the Dean of Men for permission to hold their spring dance in a nearby city; thus they would not have to drive long distances to call for and return their dates.
Comment	In the poor example the writer needlessly and awkwardly shifts from the active to the passive voice in the second independent clause. In the corrected version he avoids this problem by making *they* the active subject of the second independent clause.

If you try hard to make your sentences and paragraphs parallel and consistent in point of view by avoiding the pitfalls and following the positive principles we have suggested, your writing should improve in style as well as in clarity.

EXERCISE 41

Read each statement carefully; then decide whether it is correct or contains an error in sentence structure. No statement contains more than one error. Indicate your decision by placing the appropriate symbol in the left-hand column next to the statement.

C	*Correct*
Frag.	*Sentence Fragment*
R.T.	*Run-Together Sentence*
C.S.	*Comma Splice*
F.R.	*Faulty Pronoun Reference*
F.P.	*Faulty Parallelism*

_____ 1. All types of weapons from guns to meat cleavers.

_____ 2. I have returned the questionnaire to my local draft board.

_____ 3. I enjoy the summer very much, for you have a chance to get needed exercise.

_____ 4. In college a student must pay close attention, because they generally cover the material only once.

_____ 5. My months in Africa were most productive, the natives helped me in every way possible.

_____ 6. Along with a few candy bars that some of us were fortunate enough to have.

_____ 7. As I walked in the stadium, I slipped on the wet pavement.

_____ 8. Sometimes Mrs. Jones was sarcastic however generally she was friendly and considerate.

_____ 9. He was intelligent, conscientious, and had a great deal of determination.

_____ 10. Gather all the experience you can someday you may be a famous columnist.

_____ 11. His ability to control children and being a versatile athlete made him an excellent playground instructor.

_____ 12. I hope to spend the summer working at a resort in New England.

_____ 13. Our teacher never pampered us or loaded us with busy work. This actually helped us to develop our talents.

_____ 14. Joe quit college to take a regular job, several years later he returned to Western State as a full-time student.

_____ 15. Not only is he considerate but also cooperative.

EXERCISE 42

Read each statement carefully; then decide whether it is correct or contains an error in sentence structure. No statement contains more than one error. Indicate your decision by placing the appropriate symbol in the left-hand column next to the statement.

    C   *Correct*
    Frag.   *Sentence Fragment*
    R.T.   *Run-Together Sentence*
    C.S.   *Comma Splice*
    F.R.   *Faulty Pronoun Reference*
    F.P.   *Faulty Parallelism*

_____ 1. Although the international situation has never been more explosive.

_____ 2. Most great literature is autobiographical, if one is true to his experience he is likely to write a readable story.

_____ 3. Many aspiring writers are compulsive and impatient.

_____ 4. The Secretary of State is already well known in other countries and has won respect.

_____ 5. Mr. Jones was sixty-three years old when I had him for a teacher he is now sixty-nine.

_____ 6. Not only was he friendly but also helpful.

_____ 7. Because I think you have much natural talent.

_____ 8. The hood of the car is built square like the hoods of today's jeeps, making the parts under the hood more accessible.

_____ 9. Although I highly regard Centerville College, I would prefer to attend a larger school in a more cosmopolitan city, therefore, I have sent my application to Columbia University.

_____ 10. The professor removed his roll book from his briefcase and called the names of the students.

_____ 11. That I have the experience and determination to do an excellent job for your company.

_____ 12. Jones is better qualified to give aid, advise, and to deal with international problems.

———————— 13. Price has traveled extensively in France; he knows how they feel toward the United States.

———————— 14. Received your letter today and thought I better rush you a quick reply.

———————— 15. I am convinced that most of the work is done unconsciously thus an hour in the morning to write and an hour in the evening to rewrite should get the job done easily.

EXERCISE 43

Read each statement carefully; then decide whether it is correct or contains an error in sentence structure. No statement contains more than one error. Indicate your decision by placing the appropriate symbol in the left-hand column next to the statement.

C   *Correct*
Frag.   *Sentence Fragment*
R.T.   *Run-Together Sentence*
C.S.   *Comma Splice*
F.R.   *Faulty Pronoun Reference*
F.P.   *Faulty Parallelism*

_____   1. In college a student encounters many distractions and he must use much determination to succeed.

_____   2. Not only was he intelligent but also considerate of others.

_____   3. I am sending you several books that you should find readable and stimulating.

_____   4. Delinquents often come from homes that are broken by death, divorce, illness, or other causes. This proves that childhood influences are extremely important.

_____   5. After the cast was removed I tried to use my right hand and I was amazed that I could write better with my left hand than with my right.

_____   6. The man who influenced the development of music more than any other person.

_____   7. Blind people have the same feelings and ambitions as those who can see; however, it requires a great effort and a strong personality.

_____   8. Tom enjoys going to the race track around dawn and watching the horses get their morning exercise.

_____   9. The next day I drove the car once more before telling them that I would be interested in buying it.

_____   10. To determine whether or not a four-day work week would cause hardships.

_____   11. The sun was shining brightly, however the courts were still too wet for play.

_____ 12. I attended a military academy where you lived and worked around your teachers most of the time.

_____ 13. Television is playing an important role in education today. They now have television classes to replace regular classes.

_____ 14. The first step which will be the buying and condemnation of the land.

_____ 15. These socially insecure people are eager to be seen with the right people and going to the right places.

EXERCISE 44

Read each statement carefully; then decide whether it is correct or contains an error in sentence structure. No statement contains more than one error. Indicate your decision by placing the appropriate symbol in the left-hand column next to the statement.

C   *Correct*
Frag.   *Sentence Fragment*
R.T.   *Run-Together Sentence*
C.S.   *Comma Splice*
F.R.   *Faulty Pronoun Reference*
F.P.   *Faulty Parallelism*

_____ 1. The purchasing agent seemed enthusiastic so perhaps we shall soon receive an order.

_____ 2. Taking notes from TV lectures and working them into an outline benefits high school students. This helps them to prepare for the college method of instruction.

_____ 3. He was friendly, cooperative, and a very good coach.

_____ 4. Mr. Doran thinks the book will be a success, because the author simplifies a complex subject.

_____ 5. Since it is wise to keep a written record of memorable experiences in your life.

_____ 6. I am sorry that I cannot be more definite about an order, however I will let you know as soon as possible.

_____ 7. Not only was he dishonest with others but also with himself.

_____ 8. Finally getting organized after a rather hectic two weeks, moving to a new city, and becoming adjusted to college.

_____ 9. Educational television must be effective; otherwise, they would not use it in the schools.

_____ 10. Fools learn from their own mistakes, wise men learn from the mistakes of others.

_____ 11. I practiced backing, parking, and how to make a good smooth start.

_____ 12. We decided that a trip to California would be educational so we made plans to leave the next Monday.

_____ 13. To help develop new fuels or a new way to power ships of all kinds.

_____ 14. Can anyone watch a blazing sunrise with its promise of a new day and still believe it is just an accident?

_____ 15. The books and supplies of a college student are quite expensive.

EXERCISE 45

Read each statement carefully; then decide whether it is correct or contains an error in sentence structure. No statement contains more than one error. Indicate your decision by placing the appropriate symbol in the left-hand column next to the statement.

C   *Correct*
Frag.   *Sentence Fragment*
R.T.   *Run-Together Sentence*
C.S.   *Comma Splice*
F.R.   *Faulty Pronoun Reference*
F.P.   *Faulty Parallelism*

_____ 1. Life had taught me a unique lesson consequently I wanted to share my experience with others.

_____ 2. When I received word that a job was available, I had to tell them about my school plans.

_____ 3. Mr. Wallace was my favorite high school teacher because he was intelligent, friendly, and a boating enthusiast.

_____ 4. The tornado warnings were broadcast, however the storm by-passed the city.

_____ 5. Hoping I have a chance to drop by and have a chat with you.

_____ 6. I certainly enjoyed talking with you perhaps our paths may cross again someday.

_____ 7. The center will consist of hospitals, doctors' offices, and pharmacies. This means one location for all medical needs.

_____ 8. Her written assignments showed originality, maturity, and were letter perfect.

_____ 9. Although it is possible that I might take a trip to California next summer.

_____ 10. Sorority activities will keep me busy and on the run. This will take up most of my spare time in college.

_____ 11. Not only was he handsome but also rich.

_____ 12. I gained my knowledge about cars by watching other people work on them.

_____ 13. My future is as uncertain as the weather, my luck may change overnight.

_____ 14. She has a pleasant manner, a winning smile, and a cheerful sense of humor.

_____ 15. Since he felt confident that his education and experience would give him the background to do an effective job.

Lesson 12

Correct Usage

The labels *correct usage* and *incorrect usage* can be applied to almost any aspect of writing, but as technical grammatical terms they have more definite meanings. In a broad sense they denote the appropriateness of the writer's language to the occasion. And in their most restricted sense they refer to the rightness or wrongness of language as established by convention. You may gain a clearer understanding of the term *usage* according to this last definition by judging which of the alternate forms in the following sentences are correct.

> I think I'll *lay* down and take a nap.
> I think I'll *lie* down and take a nap.
>
> I *seen* Tom at the race track last Saturday.
> I *saw* Tom at the race track last Saturday.
>
> Tom *don't* care what anybody thinks.
> Tom *doesn't* care what anybody thinks.
>
> She drives *bad*.
> She drives *badly*.
>
> He plays the guitar real *good*.
> He plays the guitar *well*.

Me and *him* went to the game together.
He and *I* went to the game together.

The argument was between Harry and *I.*
The argument was between Harry and *me.*

The incorrect usage found in the above examples seldom appears in compositions (except as deliberate distortions for special effects), because most of the people who use substandard English do very little writing. Yet now and then such illiterate forms as *I have went* or *he don't* appear in college themes. More frequently, though, they are heard or overheard in conversations. In either case the reader or listener should feel concern for the student who uses these constructions, for he has a serious problem that has probably caused him painful embarrassment in his social life, that probably will be a serious handicap in most white-collar jobs, and that very likely will present difficulties in his scholastic writing.

You have probably already discovered the enormous snobbery that surrounds the use of language. Often people are accepted or rejected because of the way they speak. Although this attitude may imply a lack of charity, it also reflects a degree of sound logic; for illiterate, sloppy, careless speech may reflect other kinds of carelessness. Most cultivated people would rather associate with friends who speak their own language—the accepted diction of the educated class—rather than substandard language.

To improve poor grammar, try adding new words and vivid expressions to your language by borrowing from published writers. Having a set system such as reading one first-rate essay each week for the purpose of finding twenty-five or thirty or forty precise words and recording them (in addition to the phrase or sentence) in a notebook or on small cards, and studying the material regularly will do wonders to improve your language skill. If you read the biographies of successful writers you will find that many of them improved their style by imitating other writers. As with playing a trumpet, before something comes out you have to put something in. The students who write well usually have read a great deal. So as you read be on the lookout for vivid words and phrases and make an effort to put them on the tip of your tongue when you speak and at your finger tips when you write. The improvement of your language ability, then, as a way to better your social life, prepare for a career, and improve your college writing depends not only on avoiding mistakes but on broadening your knowledge of correct usage.

Our final consideration of usage relates to the appropriateness of the language to the occasion. We have touched upon this aspect in the sections on deadwood, inflated diction, weak words, and, by implication, in all the other sections of this book.

To give you a brief picture of how language is used in our society, we shall resort to an analogy that you may use as a hook for the ideas. The use of language has often been compared to the clothes people wear. This comparison, although by no means perfect, may be more helpful than an abstract definition in illustrating how language functions. Although we could use women's clothes in our analogy, we believe the relationship will be clearer if we use men's apparel.

Starting at the top, *formal language* might be compared to the white tie and tails a man would wear on a very formal occasion. This type is used in some scholarly writing, but there is a trend away from its loftiness even in academic circles. In your college writing you may never be asked to use this mode of expression. Some of its distinguishing qualities are an impersonal tone, the use of the passive voice, long and complicated sentence structure, and an elevated or technical vocabulary.

Next we have *semiformal language* that might be compared to the conventional tuxedo or perhaps to the dark suit, white shirt, and conservative tie a man might wear to a semiformal dance. This is the style you will generally be expected to use in your college writing and in your professional correspondence. We have explained some of the features of semiformal writing in the earlier sections: the pruning of deadwood, the removal of inflated diction, the rejection of weak words, and the elimination of clichés.

Next in the language scale comes *informal writing*, which might be compared to slacks, sport shirt, and sweater or colorful sport jacket worn with contrasting trousers. This is the style you might be asked to use in a basic composition course in which your themes are based on personal experience, or the diction you would use in writing a letter to a close friend. Some of the marks of informal writing are the use of contractions, the use of weak or overemphatic words, the clever use of slang, and the use of clichés for an ironic effect. But in most of your writing assignments, you will be expected to use the semiformal mode rather than the breezy, informal language you would use in a letter to a personal friend.

In the same class with informal writing is *colloquial* language, which is used by educated people in their everyday speech. Some people have the mistaken notion that the term *colloquial* denotes substandard language; however, *colloquial* when correctly used means the type of language used in ordinary speech, which in many respects is similar to informal writing.

On the lowest end of the scale is *substandard* or *vulgate*. In our analogy we might compare substandard language to the blue chambray shirt and dungarees of the working man, for, since his job does not require the more sophisticated speech, the "blue collar" rather than the "white collar" worker perhaps more often uses substandard forms similar to those listed at the beginning of this section: I seen . . . Tom don't . . . drives bad . . . plays the guitar real good . . . me and him went, etc.

In attempting to classify language, we should not think for a moment that these distinctions are sharp and clear. For the various categories of language have more similarities than differences. Nor should we mistakenly conclude that the cultural level of a person's language is necessarily an index of his intelligence nor an indication of his worth. The automobile mechanic who says *I seen* may be a mechanical genius and an excellent person in every respect. And he may have no problems at all that stem from the language he uses. On the other hand, he may be judged as inferior on the basis of his language, even though he is actually superior in native ability and intelligence. Therefore, it would be unwise for you as a college student to underestimate the importance of avoiding sub-standard language forms if you want to avoid trouble and embarrassment. And if you plan a career in business or in one of the professions it is of course essential that you avoid these substandard forms.

In the Glossary that follows you will find an alphabetized list of words that are commonly misused in speech and writing. Also you will find words that are frequently misspelled because they sound the same or look the same. The list is not very long, and you should be able to master it in a short time if you are convinced of the necessity of *correct usage* not only in your scholastic work but also in your social life and profession.

Glossary of Usage

The quoted definitions are taken from the *Standard College Dictionary*, Copyright 1966 by Funk & Wagnalls.[1]

Accept is a verb that means "to receive with favor, willingness, or consent."

> He decided to *accept* the offer from General Motors rather than go to graduate school.

Except is generally used as a preposition to mean "with the exclusion or omission of."

> Everyone at the meeting voted for the proposal *except* David and me.

Affect is a verb that means to influence.

Effect is a verb that means "to bring about; produce as a result; cause."

> *Incorrect*　The Constitutional Revision Committee was able to *affect* most of the changes it had recommended.
>
> *Correct*　The Constitutional Revision Committee was able to *effect* most of the changes it had recommended.

Effect is also a noun that means a result.

> *Incorrect*　The weather did not *effect* his moods.
> *Correct*　The weather did not *affect* his moods.
>
> *Incorrect*　The *affect* of atomic radiation on future generations is not yet known.
> *Correct*　The *effect* of atomic radiation on future generations is not yet known.

Ain't is used by people from diversified backgrounds as a contraction of *am not.* Sometimes *ain't* is used by well-educated persons to achieve a facetious or ironic

[1]Definitions quoted by permission from Funk & Wagnalls *Standard*® *College Dictionary*, copyrigh 1966 by Funk & Wagnalls, a division of Reader's Digest Books, Inc.

effect, the user assuming that the listener or reader takes for granted that the user knows *ain't* is ungrammatical. *Ain't* used carelessly or through ignorance in a business or social situation where the word is normally taboo, is almost certain to bring judgment upon the user as being unlettered.

All right means satisfactory or correct.

Alright is a deviant form of *all right.* The form *alright* is "a spelling not yet considered acceptable."

Already means "before or by this time or the time mentioned."

> *Correct*   The meeting had *already* started by the time I arrived.

All ready means completely ready.

> *Correct*   The players were *all ready* for the second half after their rest in the dressing room.

All together means all in one place.

> *Correct*   We were *all together,* sitting at the picnic table, when the rain began to fall.

Altogether means "completely, wholly."

> *Correct*   I am not *altogether* sure what you mean by that remark.

bad/badly
Bad and *badly* are often confused even by literate people who desire to use correct English. *Bad* should be used as an adjective to describe how one feels physically. *Badly* is an adverb and should describe a type of action.

> *Incorrect*   I feel *badly.*
> *Correct*   I feel *bad.*
>
> *Incorrect*   She drives *bad.*
> *Correct*   She drives *badly.*

complement/compliment
Complement means "that which fills up or completes a thing."

> *Correct*   Her modish red hat *complements* her stylish black dress.

Compliment means "an expression of admiration, praise, or congratulation."

> *Correct*   Several people who heard the speech *complimented* him on his courage to take a firm stand on the controversial subject.

council/counsel
Council is a noun that means "an assembly of persons convened for consultation or deliberation."

> *Correct*   The city *council* met every Thursday evening.

Counsel when used as a noun means "mutual exchange of advice, opinions, etc., consultation." When used as a verb, *counsel* means "to give advice to; to advise."

Correct   Brown followed the *counsel* of his lawyer and paid the fine without complaint.

Correct   The faculty adviser *counseled* the new student to take English and mathematics the first quarter.

don't/doesn't

The use of don't for doesn't (the plural verb with the singular subject) is widespread in American society, but should be scrupulously avoided by careful speakers and writers, because this usage is considered substandard English and unacceptable by the educated class.

Incorrect   He *don't* live here.
Correct   He *doesn't* live here.

Incorrect   She *don't* belong to a sorority.
Correct   She *doesn't* belong to a sorority.

effect—see *affect*

except—see *accept*

farther/further

Use *farther* when referring to distance that can be measured.

Correct   Joe lives *farther* down the street than Nick.

Use *further* when speaking of intangible distance or difference in degree.

Correct   Because he has a college education, Jack should go *further* in business than his brother who does not have a college degree.

fewer/less

Fewer should be used in referring to objects that can be counted.

Correct   Fewer players were used in the game today than last Saturday.

Less is used when referring to material that cannot be counted.

Correct   *Less* grain was harvested today than yesterday.

good/well

Good is used correctly as a predicate adjective after verbs of hearing, seeing, smelling, tasting, etc., to qualify the subject. If you have trouble understanding the term *predicate adjective* recall for a moment that an adjective is a word that describes or limits a noun or pronoun. The term *predicate* is another word for verb. Although the predicate adjective follows the verb, it does not modify the verb as would an adverb (like *walks slowly*) but describes the subject of the verb as in the following sentence: The flowers smell sweet.

Incorrect   He sings *good.*
Correct   He sings *well.*

Well is generally used as an adverb.

Correct   The quarterback kicks and passes *well.*

Well may be used as an adjective in reference to the state of health of a person.

> *Correct*   Gates is not feeling *well* today.

I/me

Confusion sometimes occurs in the use of *I* and *me* when the pronoun *you* or a proper noun comes between the preposition and the second pronoun object. The correct form of the second pronoun can often be determined by reversing the words that follow the preposition and seeing and hearing (in your mind's ear) if the pronoun looks and sounds correct, as we have done in the following examples.

> *Incorrect*   The final one-hundred-yard dash was between *Bill* and *I.*
> *Test*   The final one-hundred-yard dash was between (*I* or *me*) and Bill.
> *Correct*   The final one-hundred-yard dash was between *Bill* and *me.*

> *Incorrect*   Just between *you* and *I,* the contract has already been awarded.
> *Test*   Just between (*I* or *me*) and *you,* the contract has already been awarded.
> *Correct*   Just between *you* and *me,* the contract has already been awarded.

its/it's

The possessive pronoun *its* is never written with an apostrophe.

> *Correct*   The dog wagged *its* tail.

It is sometimes is contracted to *it's* in informal writing.

> *Correct*   *It's* too bad that you won't be able to go home this weekend.

imply/infer

Imply means "to indicate or suggest without stating."

> *Correct*   I was not certain what his tone of voice *implied.*

Infer means "to derive by reasoning; conclude or accept from evidence or premises."

> *Correct*   "Gentlemen of the jury, from the evidence presented, the *inference* should be perfectly clear. The defendant is obviously guilty."

lay (laying)/lie (lying)

Lay means to place. *Laying* means placing.

> *Correct*   *Lay* the book on the table.
> *Correct*   He was *laying* the book on the table when I came in.

Lie means to take or assume a position. *Lying* means being in a position.

> *Correct*   The doctor told him to *lie* on the couch.
> *Correct*   The patient was *lying* on the couch when the doctor returned.

lay/laid

Lay (not *laid*) is the past tense of *lie.*
Laid is the past tense of *lay.*

> *Correct*   He *lay* on the couch for several minutes before the doctor returned.
> *Correct*   He *laid* the book on the table.

less—see *fewer*

like/as if or **as though**
Like should be used as a preposition.

> *Correct*   He runs *like* a deer.

As if or *as though* should be used as a conjunction to introduce a clause.

> *Correct*   His skin looked *as if* he had been in the sun all day.

lead/led
The principal parts of the verb *lead* are *lead, led, have led.* Students sometime erroneously use *lead* instead of *led* for the past tense form.

> *Correct*   He was asked to *lead* the group to their new quarters.
> *Correct*   He *led* the horse from the paddock to the starting gate.
> *Correct*   For three straight years they *have led* the Community Chest drive.

leave/let
Leave means "to allow to remain behind or in a specified place, condition, etc."

> *Correct*   You can *leave* your books here. No one will bother them.

Let means "to allow; permit."

> *Correct*   *Let* us take this route for a change.

lose/loose
Lose means "to part with, as by accident or negligence, and be unable to find."

> *Correct*   We hated to *lose* the money.

Loose means "not fastened or confined."

> *Correct*   You better cut off that *loose* button before you *lose* it.

principal/principle
Principal as an adjective means "first in rank, character, or importance."

> *Correct*   The *principal* speaker was Dr. Jarvis.

Principal as a noun means "one who takes a leading part or who is a leader or chief in some action."

> *Correct*   Mr. Jacobs is the *principal* of our high school.

Principle as a noun means "a general truth or law, basic to other truths."

> *Correct*   He follows the *principle* that one should treat everyone with consideration and respect.

quiet/quite
Quiet means "making little or no noise."

> *Correct*   Let's study in the library where it is *quiet.*

Quite means "to the fullest extent; totally."

> *Correct*   I am *quite* certain I can be there by noon.

rise/raise

Rise, rose, risen is an intransitive verb (does not take an object) that means "to move upward."

> *Correct* I *rise* every morning at seven.
> *Correct* He *rose* from his chair and turned off the radio.
> *Correct* He *has risen* at the same time every morning since he started his new job.

Raise, raised, raised is a transitive verb (takes an object) that means "to cause to move upward or to a higher level."

> *Correct* He *raised* the window because the room was stuffy.
> *Correct* It is stuffy in here. Would you please *raise* the window?
> *Correct* He *has raised* the curtain for every performance of the Broadway musical.

sure/surely

Sure means "free from doubt; certain."

> *Correct* I am *sure* that I can be there.

Surely means "without doubt; certainly."

> *Correct* I am *surely* glad we took this route.

that/which

That is used to refer to people, animals, or inanimate objects. *Which* refers only to the latter two.

> *Incorrect* The beggar *which* stopped me was obviously drunk.
> *Correct* The beggar *that* (or *who*) stopped me was obviously drunk.
> *Correct* The bar *which* you passed is his favorite.

their/there/they're

Their is the possessive case of *they.*

> *Correct* They hung *their* coats in the closet.

There is an adverb that means "in, at, or about that place." *There* and *here* are comparable in form and function.

> *Correct* He arrived *there* before his friends. He came *here* to find a job.

They're is a contraction of *they are.* Contractions as a general rule should be avoided in college expository writing.

> *Correct* *They're* going to Chicago this weekend to do their Christmas shopping.

to/too

Students frequently use *to* when *too* is needed.
To is the sign of the infinitive.

> *Correct* I like *to* hunt and *to* fish.

To is also used as a preposition.

> *Correct* The award was given *to* Joe and me.

Too is properly used as an adverb to mean likewise or also, more than enough.

> *Correct*   Bruce, *too,* was in favor of the proposed change.
> *Correct*   Ralph was *too* tired to go to the movie after practicing football all afternoon.

weather/whether

Weather means "the general atmospheric condition. . . ."

> *Correct*   The *weather* today is ideal for boating.

Whether means "if it be the case that."

> *Correct*   *Whether* Tom helps me or not, I still intend to overhaul the motor.

well—see *good*

whose/who's

Whose is the possessive case of *who.*

> *Correct*   *Whose* car is blocking the driveway?

Who's is the contraction for *who is.*

> *Correct*   *Who's* going to be the first to volunteer to give a pint of blood?

who/whom

When in doubt as whether to use *who* or *whom,* try this substitution test. *Who* is in the same case as *she, he, it, they. Whom* is in the same case as *her, him, them.*

> *Problem*   *(Who* or *whom)* is at the door?
> *Test*   *He* or *him* is at the door?
> *Correct*   *Who* is at the door?
>
> *Problem*   He pondered a long time, trying to decide *(who* or *whom)* to invite.
> *Test*   . . . trying to decide to invite *they* or *them*?
> *Correct*   He pondered a long time, trying to decide *whom* to invite.

EXERCISE 46

Read each sentence carefully and decide which of the italicized words in parentheses is correct. Then write your preference in the left-hand column next to the corresponding number.

_____ 1. As Helen picked up her purse, she noticed her keys (*lying-laying*) on the dresser.

_____ 2. I am not (*all together-altogether*) convinced that he is capable of holding the office.

_____ 3. Although Gordon has a pleasing personality, he usually will not (*accept-except*) responsibility; therefore, I do not think he would make an effective officer.

_____ 4. We should pick a man (*who-whom*) is best qualified for the job.

_____ 5. He seemed embarrassed over the (*complement-compliment*) his friends paid him.

_____ 6. The horror movie had no (*affect-effect*) on me.

_____ 7. I felt so (*bad-badly*) I decided to stay home from work.

_____ 8. (*Let-leave*) us go upstairs and see if the Dean is in his office.

_____ 9. Although he is broad-minded and tolerant, he will not compromise his (*principles-principals*) on certain issues.

_____ 10. They parked (*their-there-they're*) cars in front of the Student Union Building.

_____ 11. I hope we do not (*lose-loose*) the game Saturday.

_____ 12. Mr. Elder, the (*principal-principle*) of our high school, is a man of high intelligence and broad sympathies.

_____ 13. By the time we reached Nashville, the sun had (*already-all ready*) disappeared behind the horizon.

_____ 14. Harper was elected to the Student (*Counsel-Council*) in spite of his radical ideas.

_____ 15. I am (*sure-surely*) glad that you got the promotion.

_____ 16. She decided to (*lay-lie*) on the beach and try to get a good sun tan.

EXERCISE 47

Read each sentence carefully and decide which of the italicized words in parentheses is correct. Then write your preference in the left-hand column next to the corresponding number.

_____ 1. The funeral procession was *(lead-led)* by a motorcycle policeman.

_____ 2. Now let us sing the song *(altogether-all together)* in a loud, clear voice.

_____ 3. Marion *(raises-rises)* every morning at the same hour.

_____ 4. The rattle was caused by a *(lose-loose)* shock absorber.

_____ 5. The Director of the Youth Club *(counciled-counseled)* the two boys after their argument on the basketball court.

_____ 6. If *(their-there-they're)* to arrive on time, they had better leave the house within the next few minutes.

_____ 7. He asked me *(who's-whose)* place I was taking.

_____ 8. After arranging his data in logical order, he stated his first *(implication-inference)*.

_____ 9. *(Whether-Weather)* or not I go to the game, depends upon the work I have to do this weekend.

_____ 10. Harry lives *(farther-further)* down the street than I.

_____ 11. Begley plays the piano *(good-well)* despite the fact that he does not read music.

_____ 12. He is not the candidate for *(who-whom)* I would vote.

_____ 13. Your answer is *(all right-alright)*, but you could add a few more details.

_____ 14. After I listened to the President on the radio, I felt *(as if-like)* I should take more interest in foreign affairs.

_____ 15. We should try to find a *(quite-quiet)* motel away from the main highway.

_____ 16. You can *(lay-lie)* in the sun all day.

EXERCISE 48

Read each sentence carefully and decide which of the italicized words in parentheses is correct. Then write your preference in the left-hand column next to the corresponding number.

_____ 1. You can *(sit-set)* down on the ground and watch the squirrels gather food for the winter.

_____ 2. The cat arched *(it's-its)* back when the dog came near the fence.

_____ 3. I have great respect for the boys *(which-who)* enlist in the armed forces.

_____ 4. Mr. Pierce wrote a letter *(to-too-two)* my sister and me.

_____ 5. A parked car on a busy avenue is an ideal place to *(set-sit)* and observe people.

_____ 6. The discussion between John and *(I-me)* lasted until midnight.

_____ 7. Her chic red hat *(compliments-complements)* her stylish black dress.

_____ 8. I *(sure-surely)* wish I could go to Florida during the spring vacation.

_____ 9. The student *(which-who)* always watches television will not have much time to read.

_____ 10. Although he is improving, at present he plays the piano *(bad-badly)*.

_____ 11. Gruber *(raised-rose)* from his chair and closed the door.

_____ 12. Freedom from want in old age is the *(principle-principal)* aim of Social Security.

_____ 13. If we get *(their-there-they're)* before you, we will wait for you in the lobby.

_____ 14. The *(whether-weather)* is quite warm for this time of year.

_____ 15. Clayton has a bad cold. He does not feel
(well-good) today.

_____ 16. *(Whose-Who's)* the man in the dark blue suit?

EXERCISE 49

Read each sentence carefully and decide which of the italicized words in parentheses is correct. Then write your preference in the left-hand column next to the corresponding number.

_____ 1. *(Its-It's)* my prediction that we should win the game by at least two touchdowns.

_____ 2. He was not *(affected-effected)* by the advice of his parents.

_____ 3. Of all the candidates, I do not believe anyone is qualified for the post *(accept-except)* Allen.

_____ 4. Do you mean to *(infer-imply)* that you think I am wrong?

_____ 5. Douglas will probably go *(further-farther)* in life than his brother.

_____ 6. In this country one has the privilege to vote for the man *(who-whom)* he favors.

_____ 7. When we arrived at Great Lakes, the petty officer in charge of our group *(lead-led)* us to the receiving building.

_____ 8. The argument between Ted and *(I-me)* was settled by the coach.

_____ 9. I am *(quite-quiet)* convinced that Holloway is guilty.

_____ 10. Sally *(laid-lay)* on the beach an hour before she entered the water.

_____ 11. The teacher *(who-whom)* I liked best was Mr. Graham.

_____ 12. There were *(less-fewer)* spectators at the game this Saturday than last.

_____ 13. I am *(to-too-two)* tired to go to the movies.

_____ 14. She had been *(lying-laying)* on the beach for an hour before her skin began to turn pink.

_____ 15. The sailors were *(already-all ready)* for liberty by the time the ship reached Trinidad.

_____ 16. When the headache persisted, Harry felt *(like-as if)* he should go to the doctor.

13

Agreement

One of the most common grammatical lapses—even among professional writers—is faulty subject-verb agreement. Many such errors result from careless proofreading or the failure to distinguish between formal (standard) and informal (colloquial) language.

Under the pressure of meeting a deadline or for some less excusable reason, we may erroneously make our verb agree with the nearest noun, which is often not the subject but the object of a phrase that modifies the true subject. The following examples will illustrate this principle.

> The poor attitude of many students (is-are) responsible for the high number of failures.
>
> Two sets of plans for building the house (was-were) submitted to the Jones family.
>
> The noises that drifted from the street below (is-are) frustrating when I am trying to study.

In the first example a careful reading of the sentence will show that *attitude* not *students* is the simple subject, requiring the singular verb *is* to agree with the singular noun *attitude*. In example two the writer might easily be led into making a mistake in agreement by relating *was* to *house* rather than correctly matching the plural verb *were* with the plural subject *sets*. The third example shows the predicate separated from the subject by a long modifier, understandably causing the writer to associate *is* with *street* rather than *are* with *noises*. Mistakes in agreement in these sentences would probably stem from lack of attention rather than ignorance of correct usage.

In writing or speaking most people do the natural thing, putting down on paper or saying whatever comes to their minds without consciously thinking about rules. However, some people have trouble writing because they are excessively rule conscious. Often the more we think about rules and their exceptions, the more we strain for an effect, causing *inflated diction* or (even worse) temporary paralysis of the fingers. On the other hand, the less we worry about rules—especially in writing the first draft—and the more we concentrate on what we are trying to say, the easier writing should be.

In college and most commercial and professional writing, though, as distinguished from informal or colloquial writing and speech, we are obliged to follow set standards, one of which is to use a singular verb with indefinite pronouns even though the pronoun may denote plurality. After you have written the first draft of your theme you should check carefully to make sure that you have not violated this principle. What form of the verb would you use in the following illustrations?

> Every one of the professors (has-have) at least five years of experience in teaching his subject on the college level.
>
> Nobody in the class (was-were) willing to serve on the committee.
>
> We decided that each of us (was-were) obliged to pay an equal amount for the broken window.

Most college English teachers would require and most college textbooks recommend the use of the singular forms (has, was, was) to agree with the indefinite pronouns even though they suggest more than one person. Besides the indefinite pronouns used in the examples already given (*everyone, nobody, each*) the following also require singular verbs for correct grammatical agreement: *anyone, either, everybody, neither, no one, somebody.*

Generally in writing what comes naturally will be right; how the sentence looks or sounds will usually tell us whether it is right or wrong. If you came across this sentence, "Joe and Mary is sure to get the leading parts in the play," you would conclude right away without an elaborate analysis that it is wrong. The sentence neither looks right nor sounds right. Immediately you realize that *are* is needed in the predicate to agree with the compound subject. However, in considering indefinite pronouns you cannot depend on your sense of sound as an infallible guide, for the forms commonly used in speech are not always acceptable in formal writing. Therefore, you will have to apply the above principles as well as other definite rules of subject-verb agreement if you are to achieve the precision that is expected of a competent writer. An understanding of the rules that follow should give you the knowledge and confidence to write sentences that are free of errors in subject-verb agreement.

Compound Subjects

1. In most constructions when the subjects (nouns or pronouns) are joined by *and* a plural verb is needed.

> Tom and his brother *were* home for the holidays.
>
> *Are* Joan and her friends going to visit New York this year?

2. When two or more singular subjects refer to the same person or thing, a singular rather than a plural verb is required.

> My friend and adviser *was* responsible for my becoming an engineer.
>
> Loafing and letting your man get behind you *is* a good way to lose the basketball game.

3. If either or both of the singular subjects are preceded by *each* or *every* to stress their individuality, the singular form of the verb is required.

> Every dog and cat in the neighborhood *was* yelping at the moon.
>
> Each boy and girl *was* given a free ticket to the zoo.

4. If the compound subjects are thought of as belonging together, a singular verb is used; if they are thought of as being separate, a plural verb is used.

> Ham and eggs *is* my favorite dish.
>
> Ham and eggs *were* purchased at the grocery by the housewife.

5. If singular compound subjects are joined by *or* or *nor* a singular verb is generally used.

> Either democracy or communism *is* the form of government that will ultimately prevail.
>
> Either Fowler or Hill *is* bound to receive the appointment to the student council.

6. If singular and plural subjects are joined by *or* or *nor* the verb agrees in number with the nearest subject.

> Neither Larry nor his classmates *were* satisfied with the way the test was given.
>
> Neither his classmates nor Larry *was* satisfied with the way the test was given.

Collective Nouns

A collective noun refers to a whole composed of individuals, nonhuman animals, or things; for example, *jury, contents, family, band, congregation, team, committee, group, herd.* As a general rule collective nouns take singular verbs: *jury was, family goes, band plays, congregation sings, team runs, committee meets, group participates.* Sometimes, though, a writer will want to emphasize plurality, the individuals within the group, and may legitimately use a plural rather than a singular verb to achieve this effect. The important point is consistency, which we shall discuss in the next section on pronoun agreement.

The jury *has* (or *have*) left the courtroom for *its* (or *their*) hotel.

His family *was* (or *were*) the first to settle in that part of the country.

The band *has* (or *have*) assembled at the end of the playing field.

The contents of her purse *was* (or *were*) spilled onto the floor.

Separated Subjects

Careful writers draw a distinction between compound subjects and separated subjects (sometimes called parenthetical expressions). As previously stated, compound subjects joined by *and* need a plural verb: Tom and his brother *were* members of the Boy Scouts. However, if *his brother* had been preceded by *along with, as well as, together with,* etc., rather than *and* a singular verb would have been required.

Tom as well as his brother *belongs* to the Boy Scouts.

The President, along with his cabinet members, *had* his picture taken on the lawn in front of the White House.

Every morning the manager, together with several of his clerks, *goes* to the restaurant for a cup of coffee.

The Secretary of State in addition to his assistants *was* present at the news conference.

Delayed Subjects

Frequently (all too frequently) student writers begin sentences with *There is* or *There are*, which can easily lead to faulty subject-verb agreement. This type of error usually results from confusing *there* with the subject. *There* in its ordinary usage is an adverb; thus the simple subject is removed from its regular place in the sentence (before the verb) to a point that often causes faulty noun-verb agreement. If you use *there is* or *there are* you should double check to make sure you have used the correct form of the verb.

There *are* (not *is*) a cow, two horses, and a mule in the pasture.

There *have* (not *has*) never been any charges brought against him during his term in office.

Nouns That Are Plural in Form but Singular in Meaning

Following the common-sense principle of *How does it sound?* will usually solve this problem. Should you write *A thousand dollars* is *a lot of money* or *A thousand dollars* are *a lot of money*? Even though *dollars* is plural our common sense tells us to use a singular verb. Many other words in the English language are plural in form but singular in meaning, taking a singular rather than a plural verb: *economics, ethics, mathematics, measles, mumps, news, physics, politics,* etc.

> Economics *is* the study of business and commerce.
>
> Mathematics *is* my favorite subject.
>
> Measles *is* the only childhood disease I haven't had.
>
> The news for the most part *is* good.

Singular or Plural Verbs Used with Relative Pronouns

Considering grammar, as such, of less importance than writing, we suggest that you not worry about this principle until you write your final draft or proofread your finished theme. Relative pronouns usually refer to the nearest noun (not necessarily the subject of the sentence). Consequently, a relative pronoun is singular or plural according to the number of its antecedent; this relationship determines the subject-verb agreement pattern. Let us consider these examples:

> Brucker is one of those people who (is–are) always helping someone else.
>
> Jones and Smith are like the fellow who (throws–throw) the baby out with the bath water.

In the first example *who* refers to *people*, making *who* plural and requiring *are* for correct pronoun-verb agreement. In the second example *who* refers to *fellow*, making *who* singular and requiring *is* for correct pronoun-verb agreement.

EXERCISE 50

Consider the subject-verb relationship in each of the following sentences. Then decide which form of the verb is correct and indicate your choice by writing the verb in the column to the left of the number.

_____ 1. The suggestion that he offered to solve the financial problems (is–are) the best I have heard.

_____ 2. There (is–are) in the opinion of the experts one factor that might cause him to change his mind.

_____ 3. The congregation (sings–sing) the songs chosen by its pastor.

_____ 4. Economy as well as looks (is–are) the reason many people buy compact cars.

_____ 5. Each soldier and sailor (was–were) given a ticket to one of the parties.

_____ 6. My friend and colleague (was–were) waiting for me when my plane landed in New York.

_____ 7. The team (is–are) inspired by their coach.

_____ 8. The going-away party that was sponsored by his fellow workers (was–were) a wonderful gesture of friendship.

_____ 9. Anyone who studies consistently (is–are) almost bound to pass the course.

_____ 10. Scotch and soda (is–are) preferred by many men.

_____ 11. Everyone who desires to pick up his tickets (is–are) asked to remain after class.

_____ 12. (Does–Do) either of the men have a place to stay?

_____ 13. Joan as well as her sister (was–were) an honor student.

_____ 14. There (is–are) to be at least fifty couples at the dance.

_____ 15. Anybody in the class (is–are) eligible to try for the scholarship.

_____ 16. Mathematics (is–are) required in the freshman and sophomore years.

_____ 17. The space capsule in addition to the booster (was–were) on display.

_____ 18. A thousand dollars (is–are) a lot of money.

_____ 19. A check for the hotel rooms used by the delegates (was–were) sent to the local chairman.

_____ 20. Each of the girls (is–are) responsible for part of the household duties.

EXERCISE 51

Consider the subject-verb relationship in each of the following sentences. Then decide which form of the verb is correct, and indicate your choice by writing the verb in the column to the left of the number.

_____ 1. Neither Jane nor her sorority sisters (was–were) pleased with the outcome of the contest.

_____ 2. There (comes–come) the Governor and his assistants.

_____ 3. Each of the salesmen (decides–decide) what days he will be out of town.

_____ 4. Hines and Lawson are like the fellow who (whistles–whistle) in the graveyard.

_____ 5. The President, along with the Deans and the Board of Directors, (was–were) on the platform.

_____ 6. The ringing of the bells (indicates–indicate) the start of a new class period.

_____ 7. The herd of cattle (satisfies–satisfy) their thirst by drinking from the pond.

_____ 8. (Does–Do) everybody understand the question?

_____ 9. Bruce is one of those boys who (is–are) always complaining about their grades.

_____ 10. There (is–are) the keys to the gear lockers.

_____ 11. The organizer of the clubs (was–were) on television.

_____ 12. The horse and buggy (was–were) waiting out in front.

_____ 13. Neither her sorority sisters nor Mary (was–were) pleased with the outcome of the contest.

_____ 14. The Bishop in addition to the priests (was–were) present for the ground-breaking ceremony.

_____ 15. Neither of us (has–have) the necessary experience to fly the plane alone.

_____ 16. The group (buys–buy) their insurance from the same company.

_____ 17. A textbook that will stress the practical problems (is–are) badly needed.

_____ 18. The ethics of government (is–are) treated in a book recently published by Dr. Dulworth.

_____ 19. The manager, together with the pitcher and catcher, (was–were) arguing with the umpire.

_____ 20. The news of the fatalities (is–are) sent to every major city by the Associated Press.

Agreement of Pronoun with Antecedent

The rules governing pronoun agreement include the same principles as subject-verb agreement. Stated in capsule form, the pronoun must agree with its antecedent in person, gender, and number. What do these technical terms mean?

Antecedent—the word or words to which the pronoun refers

> *John* told the committee that he disagreed with the procedure.
> *John* is the antecedent of *he*.

Person—any one of the three relations underlying discourse

	Singular	Plural
1st (person speaking)	my	our
2nd (person spoken to)	your	your
3rd (person spoken of)	his, her, its	their

Gender—the sex (or lack of sex) of a person, animal, or thing

Masculine gender	John put *his* coat on the rack.
Feminine gender	Mary put *her* coat on the rack.
Neuter gender	The tree cast *its* shadow on the ground.

Number—whether the pronoun refers to one or more persons or things

Singular	Joyce went to see *her* adviser.
Plural	Joe and Harry went to see *their* adviser.

Indefinite Pronouns

One of the most common mistakes in pronoun reference stems from using the plural pronoun (e.g., *their* instead of *his*) to refer to indefinite pronouns that are singular in form but plural in meaning. In formal writing a singular pronoun in the appropriate gender refers to the following indefinite pronouns:

one	someone	everybody	neither
anyone	somebody	each	no one
anybody	everyone	either	nobody

Everybody gave the teacher *his* undivided attention.

Neither of the girls could do *her* best work under pressure.

Nobody would volunteer *his* time for the unpleasant job of collecting the money.

Either of the boys may jeopardize *his* future in college sports by accepting the invitation from the alumni.

Everyone agreed that *he* would give 10 percent of his December salary to the charity drive.

Each of the girls has *her* own ideas about the Christmas decorations.

Either of the teachers could have written *his* own textbook.

Note in the above examples the masculine pronoun is used when the gender could be either masculine or feminine or both: Everybody gave the teacher *his* undivided attention. Either of the teachers could have written *his* own textbook.

Collective Nouns

Collective nouns *(jury, council, committee, herd, band)* usually take singular verbs and pronouns, except when the writer wants to stress the plurality of the group. Thus the verb used with the collective noun determines the number and gender of the pronoun.

> The jury *gives its* (not *their*) decision to the judge.
>
> The city council *are* determined to enact *their* (not *its*) proposal.
>
> The committee *pleads its* (not *their*) case before the manager.
>
> The herd *are* stopping by the water hole to quench *their* (not *its*) thirst.
>
> The band *takes its* (not *their*) place at the end of the field.

In proofreading your theme, you should make sure that the verb and pronoun used with a collective noun are in the same number—singular or plural.

Compound Subjects

The same considerations that govern subject-verb agreement are applicable to pronouns that refer to compound subjects. If the subjects are joined by *and* (Earl *and* Frank) the plural form of the pronoun is generally used.

> Earl and Frank brought *their* records to the dance.
>
> Marie and Sally straightened *their* room before going to dinner.

If singular compound subjects are joined by *or* or *nor,* a singular pronoun is generally required.

> Neither Earl nor Frank would admit that *he* was wrong.
>
> Marie or Sally will be asked to present *her* plans for the dance.

If singular and plural compound subjects are joined by *or* or *nor,* the pronoun usually agrees with the nearest subject.

> Neither the house mother nor the girls *expect* to have all *their* wishes satisfied.
>
> Neither the girls nor the house mother *expects* to have all *her* wishes satisfied.
>
> Either the policemen or the detective *was* instructed to assert *his* authority.
>
> Either the detective or the policemen *were* instructed to assert *their* authority.

Relative Pronouns

The number (singular or plural) of the relative pronoun is determined by the noun to which the pronoun refers, often the object of a phrase modifying the subject—not the subject itself. We hope these examples will clarify this tricky point of grammar.

> Jones is one of those students *who* never meet *their* (not *his*) obligations.
>
> Some college students are like the man *who* thought *he* (not *they*) could get something for nothing.

In the first example the relative pronoun *who* refers to *students*—not Jones —making it plural in number and requiring *their* rather than *his* for correct pronoun agreement. In the second example the relative pronoun *who* refers to *man* —not *students*—making it singular in number and requiring *he* rather than *they* for correct pronoun agreement.

As we suggested before, you should not worry too much about these principles while writing the first draft of your theme; rather you should concentrate on what you are trying to say, expressing your ideas in clear language and avoiding flowery diction. Then after you have your thoughts down on paper you should check your composition for faulty grammar.

EXERCISE 52

Consider the pronoun-antecedent relationship in each of the following sentences. Then decide which form of the pronoun enclosed in parentheses is correct and indicate your preference by writing the pronoun in the left-hand column next to the number.

_____ 1. Every student in the class asked the coach to sign (his–their) yearbook.

_____ 2. Neither the coach nor the team members were willing to make the trip at (his–their) own expense.

_____ 3. Any girl who wants to join one of the sororities should sign (her–their) name at the bottom of the sheet.

_____ 4. Irene is like the Hollywood star who expects everyone to cater to (her–their) whims.

_____ 5. The team spends (its–their) first week of practice doing calisthenics.

_____ 6. Neither the team members nor the coach was willing to make the trip at (his–their) own expense.

_____ 7. He was one of those rare individuals who seem contented with (his–their) lot.

_____ 8. Everyone on the ship was worried that perhaps (he-they) would not return safely to port.

_____ 9. If a person will ask questions (he–they) should be able to find the lodge without any trouble.

_____ 10. The Business Club elect (its–their) officers at the first meeting of the New Year.

_____ 11. Neither the players nor the coach could control (his–their) temper.

_____ 12. Tom is one of those fellows who never express (his–their) opinion.

_____ 13. The squadron was taken to (its–their) quarters after it landed on the aircraft carrier.

_____ 14. She is one of those women who are constantly asserting (her–their) authority.

_____ 15. Someone wrote (his–their) name in the concrete before it had dried.

_____ 16. Every girl who is hired by the company is expected to furnish (her–their) own uniform.

_____ 17. The majority of the delegates cast (his–their) votes for Edward Owens.

_____ 18. Neither the coach nor the players could control (his–their) tempers.

_____ 19. Each of the girls has decided to rent (her–their) own apartment.

_____ 20. Not one of my friends is going to cast (his–their) vote for Senator Smith.

EXERCISE 53

Consider the pronoun-antecedent relationship in each of the following sentences. Then decide which form of the pronoun enclosed in parentheses is correct and indicate your preference by writing the pronoun in the left-hand column next to the number.

_____ 1. The jury voice (its–their) opinions only in closed sessions.

_____ 2. She is the type of person who knows exactly what (she wants–they want) in life.

_____ 3. Everyone felt that (his–their) short story should take the prize.

_____ 4. Neither the sergeant nor the privates would admit that (he was–they were) absent without leave.

_____ 5. The Security Council of the U.N.O. call (its–their) members into session whenever an international crisis develops.

_____ 6. The student will learn more about college life if (he has–they have) several talks with upperclassmen.

_____ 7. Many disgusted students will readily admit that the main reason for (his–their) failure is the stupidity of the teachers.

_____ 8. Neither of the senators would lend (his–their) support to the Foreign Aid Bill.

_____ 9. She is one of those women who try (her–their) best to get in the last word.

_____ 10. Both Hemingway and Fitzgerald devoted (his–their) literary talents to prose rather than poetry.

_____ 11. When a person receives instructions from his superiors, (he–they) should make every effort to carry them out.

_____ 12. The Committee on Special Events meets every Wednesday to consider (its–their) problems.

_____ 13. Tom is one of those fellows who wear (his–their) hats inside the house.

_____ 14. No solution is possible as long as everyone is determined to have (his–their) own way.

_____ 15. Sporting events and other social activities are helpful to student morale if (it is–they are) not overly stressed.

_____ 16. The herd of wild buffalo drinks (its–their) fill at the water hole.

_____ 17. A person should not put off a written assignment until the last minute if (he expects–they expect) to do a superior job.

_____ 18. He was one of those rare individuals who seem to know (his–their) way by intuition.

_____ 19. Either the policeman or the men arrested for speeding are lying in (his–their) account of the accident.

_____ 20. The band is taking (its–their) place at the end of the field.

EXERCISE 54

Consider the subject-verb or pronoun-antecedent relationship in each of the following sentences. Then decide which form of the verb or pronoun enclosed in parentheses is correct and indicate your preference by writing it in the left-hand column next to the number.

_____ 1. Mathematics, although difficult for some students, (presents–present) no challenge to Roger.

_____ 2. Neither of the pilots (is–are) experienced in night flying.

_____ 3. The Chamber of Commerce has (its–their) annual banquet at the Statler Hotel.

_____ 4. The audience (enjoys–enjoy) expressing their opinions about the play.

_____ 5. He is one of those rare individuals who (has–have) decided on a definite career.

_____ 6. The congregation at its yearly business meeting (elects–elect) ten representatives to the National Council.

_____ 7. She is one of those girls who (is–are) always late for appointments.

_____ 8. Every boy and girl (was–were) asked to comment on the value of the new regulations.

_____ 9. Either Bruce or John (is–are) bound to be elected to the student council.

_____ 10. Neither of the players (has–have) a chance to make the All-Star Team.

_____ 11. There (is–are) in the class students who have no interest in the subject.

_____ 12. My friend and severest critic (has–have) given me valuable help with the manuscript.

_____ 13. Chemistry or physics (is–are) of no great value to a student unless he intends to major in science.

_____ 14. The association of family doctors has (its–their) yearly meeting in New York.

_____ 15. Each of the board members (is–are) an official in the company.

_____ 16. Neither Helm nor his assistants (feels–feel) any responsibility for the fire.

_____ 17. Everybody who goes to the tournament will have (his–their) train fare paid by the Booster Club.

_____ 18. A person who has musical or literary talents (has–have) a good chance of getting a scholarship.

_____ 19. The bowling team holds (its–their) annual banquet at the Statler Hotel.

_____ 20. Every employee must present (his–their) badge before entering the plant.

EXERCISE 55

Consider the subject-verb or pronoun-antecedent relationship in each of the following sentences. Then decide which form of the verb or pronoun enclosed in parentheses is correct and indicate your preference by writing it in the left-hand column next to the number.

_____ 1. Everyone agreed that (he–they) would put up $100 to get the club started.

_____ 2. The members of the Chamber of Commerce (tries–try) to persuade new industry to locate in the city.

_____ 3. Every boy and girl in the band (was–were) able to make the trip.

_____ 4. Two proposals for widening the street (was–were) submitted to the Board of Aldermen.

_____ 5. The audience, as well as the actors and actresses, was generous in giving (its–their) support to the fund drive.

_____ 6. We agreed that each of us (was–were) responsible for keeping the house clean.

_____ 7. Neither Durham nor his colleagues gave (his–their) information to the Attorney General.

_____ 8. My good friend and physician (visits–visit) me every summer at my camp in Maine.

_____ 9. The bonus he received for signing the contract and his first year's salary (amounts–amount) to $100,000.

_____ 10. The audience (was–were) not reluctant to express its disapproval.

_____ 11. Jane and her sister are like the Hollywood star who (expects–expect) praise from everyone.

_____ 12. The team was escorted to the dressing room and told that (it–they) would be expected on the field in an hour.

_____ 13. Burke is one of those fellows who (knows–know) by instinct how the stock market will fluctuate.

_____ 14. Neither Combs nor his followers (offers–offer) convincing evidence.

_____ 15. The squad of policemen devote (its–their) entire attention to guarding the President.

_____ 16. There (is–are) one set of instructions for each pilot.

_____ 17. Neither the members of the board nor the chairman (was–were) available.

_____ 18. Neither of the boys could give (his–their) full support to the controversial proposal.

_____ 19. The enthusiasm of the rooters (was–were) responsible for the team's brilliant performance.

_____ 20. Every member of the committee should do (his–their) utmost to make the dance a success.

Lesson 14

Punctuation

End Punctuation

Periods are used at the end of declarative, imperative, and mildly exclamatory sentences. Moreover, a period—not a question mark—comes at the end of an indirect question.

Declarative	January has been a horrible month.
Imperative	Please shut the door.
Mildly Exclamatory	What a magnificent sunset.
Indirect Question	He asked me what road to take.

Three spaced periods (. . .) are used to indicate an omission in a quoted passage. If one or more complete sentences are omitted or if the omission comes at the beginning or end of a sentence, four periods are used: the ellipsis mark and the regular period (. . . .).

The material quoted below is from *Gulliver's Travels* by Jonathan Swift. Note that four periods are used at the end, because the entire paragraph is not quoted. Compare the second passage with the first, noting the parts that have been deleted and the ellipsis marks used to indicate the omissions.

When this adventure was at an end, I came back out of my house, having occasion for fresh air. The Emperor was already descended from the tower, and advancing on horseback towards me, which had like to have cost him dear; for the beast, though very well trained, yet wholly unused to such a sight, which appeared as if a mountain moved before him, reared on his hinder feet: but that prince, who is an excellent horseman, kept his seat, till his attendants ran in, and held the bridle, while his master had time to mount . . . .

When this adventure was at an end, I came back out of my house . . . . The Emperor was already descended from the tower, and advancing on horseback towards me, which had like to have cost him dear; for the beast . . . wholly unused to such a sight, which appeared as if a mountain moved before him, reared up on his hinder feet: but that prince . . . kept his seat, till his attendants ran in, and held the bridle, while his master had time to mount . . . .

Periods are used after abbreviations.

Names	J. B. Smith, James T. Dugan
Degrees	B.A., M.A., Ph.D.
Months	Jan., Feb., Mar.
States	Ind., Ky., Ill., Ala.
Titles	Rev., Dr., Col.
Others	Ave., St., pp., U.S.A., p.m., *ibid.*, A.D.

Names of some governmental agencies, television and radio stations, and other abbreviations are not followed by periods.

FBI	WLW	MS (manuscript)
NATO	WSM	MSS (manuscripts)
NASA	WHAS	

Question Marks

A question mark is placed at the end of a direct question.

How many couples were at the dance?

A period—not a question mark—is used to punctuate an indirect question.

Don asked me if I would help him with his algebra.

A question mark is sometimes used after an aside question interjected into a statement.

Everyone who wants to be paid—can there be anyone who doesn't?—should muster at the drill hall.

A question mark should follow a brief question at the end of a declarative sentence.

They have definitely decided to move to Boston, haven't they?

When a question mark and quotation marks fall together, the question mark goes outside the quotes if the complete statement is a direct question.

Did he say, "Who would like to try out for the play"?

He walked into the classroom and asked, "Who would like to try out for the play?"

"What time does the train leave?" he asked.

He shouted in a loud voice, "Who would like to volunteer for the drill hall detail?"

A question mark is correctly used to express uncertainty as to dates or other factual data.

The castle was destroyed in 1156 (?).

The use of a question mark after a word or phrase to achieve a humorous or ironic effect is considered poor practice.

His funny (?) stories were more effective than any sleeping pills.

Exclamation Points

The exclamation point is used after emphatic interjections and statements expressing very strong emotion.

Extra! Extra! Extra! Read all about it!

Help! Help! I'm drowning!

The comma or period—rather than the exclamation point—should be used after mild interjections and temperate exclamatory statements.

Oh, I would just as soon not go to the dance.

What a beautiful sunset.

The exclamation point should be used sparingly, only in situations where a strong emotional impact is needed. Where the exclamation point and quotation marks fall together, the exclamation point goes inside or outside the quotation marks, depending upon whether the entire statement or only the quoted words are considered exclamatory.

"Get out of those bunks!" yelled the master-at-arms.

I did not say, "Halt"!

Colons

Except to introduce a formal quotation, the colon should come at the end of a statement that can stand alone as a sentence. The colon is used to introduce a formal listing or a statement that repeats in other words or amplifies the preceding statement.

Emerson wisely observed: "The President pays dearly for his White House."

The three cars were side by side waiting for the light to change: a Rambler, a Chevrolet, and a Ford.

I used the following books in my reference paper: *The Future of an Illusion* by Sigmund Freud, *Psychoanalysis and Religion* by Erich Fromm, *A Primer of Freudian Psychology* by Calvin S. Hall, and *Psyche and Symbol* by C. G. Jung.

The sailors lay on the fantail basking in the sun: The fantail is the back end of the ship.

The colon is also used in the following situations:

After the formal salutation in a letter Dear Sir:
Dear Mr. Brown:

Between the hour and minutes in noting time 5:30 P.M.
1:20 A.M.

In Biblical references Mark 8:13–21
Luke 10:51–55

EXERCISE 56

Read the following statements carefully and insert the omitted punctuation. In some instances the wrong punctuation marks are used. Delete the erroneous mark by drawing a circle around it, and write the correct form above the circle.

1. When will the plane arrive.

2. His favorite novels are: *Moby Dick* and *Crime and Punishment.*

3. A hundred dollars. Do you think I'm a millionaire?

4. He had an appointment for 9 30 A.M.

5. Did he ask, "Who would like to volunteer for the committee?"

6. Will you please open your books to page 75?

7. My favorite colors are: red, gold, and green.

8. He asked what time we were leaving?

9. I said run not walk.

10. He asked, "What is the meaning of this uproar"?

11. The following is one of my favorite Biblical passages. "Look at the birds of the air. They neither reap nor gather into barns. Yet your heavenly Father feeds them."

12. Station W.L.W. is located in Cincinnati.

13. Did he actually say, "Who would like to take the trip with me?"

14. Who has the key to the cabinet.

15. Dr Embry gave a stimulating lecture on *Heart of Darkness.*

16. The first class petty officer shouted the following instructions. Wait on the platform for the truck to take you to your permanent barracks.

17. He quoted the following lines from *Hamlet.* "Neither a borrower nor a lender be/ for loan oft loses both self and friend."

18. The meeting will be held on Jan 15.

19. "Who would like to take the trip with me," he asked as he came in the room.

20. He asked me what road he should take to Peoria?

EXERCISE 57

Read the following statements carefully and insert the omitted punctuation. In some instances the wrong punctuation marks are used. Delete the erroneous mark by drawing a circle around it, and write the correct form above the circle.

1. This summer I read several engrossing novels; *For Whom the Bell Tolls,* *Crime and Punishment,* and *The Stranger.*

2. N.A.T.O. was established at the end of World War II.

3. The following cities are being considered as convention sites. New York, New Orleans, and San Francisco.

4. The plane taxied to the end of the runway

5. "Up on your feet—you lousy bums."

6. What a strange way to conduct a class.

7. He has his M A degree in history.

8. "Who has the answer" he asked?

9. Ouch. That blasted iron is hot.

10. The following men report to the Drill Hall. Davis, Harper, and Heiser.

11. Whoosh. Almost immediately the jet was out of sight.

12. Until recently he was an agent for the F.B.I.

13. "On the double," the sergeant shouted!

14. He gave the following directions. Turn right when you reach the crossroads; drive ten miles; turn left when you reach Route 66.

15. Oh I don't believe there's anything to worry about.

16. This is the last game of the season, isn't it.

17. The novel was written by Charles E Meyer.

18. Anyone who wants to write a longer paper—I wonder how many ambitious students are in the class—may do so.

19. The following words are used to show a logical relationship between ideas; moreover, consequently, furthermore, however, thus, hence.

20. The play began at 7–30 P.M.

EXERCISE 58

Read the following statements carefully and insert the omitted punctuation. In some instances the wrong punctuation marks are used. Delete the erroneous mark by drawing a circle around it and write the correct form above the circle.

1. The following students will be excused from class to go on the field trip. Jones, Morris, and Trapp.
2. You did ask to be excused from class, didn't you.
3. Do you think that the Russians are sincere in promoting world disarmament.
4. A quarter for a cup of coffee. That is preposterous.
5. The policy contained the following provision. No teen-ager was allowed to drive the car at any time.
6. Anyone who prefers to attend the eight o'clock class—I wonder how many early birds we have—may indicate his desire by writing his name on this sheet of paper.
7. "Oh my aching back," he shouted when he saw the work schedule the sergeant had drawn up.
8. After a month of dry weather, the rain finally came down in torrents.
9. The train departed at 8 30 P M , Eastern Standard Time.
10. "Who will be the first to volunteer," he asked?
11. Professor Carter has his PhD from Northwestern University.
12. Brrrrrr. This weather is for the Eskimos.
13. The motion to adjourn was made by J T Carter.
14. What time does the bus leave for St. Louis.
15. The following notice was written on the blackboard; The class will meet in Room 301 instead of 201.
16. Station W.W.L. has its studios in the Roosevelt Hotel in New Orleans.
17. "What is the meaning of this," he asked in a stern voice.

18. He decided to join the Navy for the following reasons. to have an opportunity to travel; to learn a trade that would help him as a civilian; to provide a monthly income for life if he served twenty years or more.

19. My favorite cities are: New Orleans, Boston, and San Francisco.

20. Tom asked me if I had ever visited Rush Street in Chicago?

Commas and Semicolons

Commas and semicolons to set off independent clauses

Commas—and sometimes semicolons—are used before coordinate conjunctions (*and, but, for, nor, or*) that join independent clauses in a compound sentence.

> The high school was located near the airport, and the loud drone of the planes was a distraction to the students and teachers.

If one or both of the independent clauses are unusually long or contain commas, a semicolon may be used at the end of the first independent clause.

> During the day, there was much activity along the main street; but at night, except for an occasional pedestrian, the sidewalks were deserted.

Semicolons are used to separate independent clauses if the second clause is introduced by an adverbial connective (*thus, hence, however, therefore, moreover, furthermore, nevertheless,* etc.). A semicolon is used also to separate independent clauses if the coordinate conjunction or the introductory adverb is omitted.

> The frigid temperature kept most of the students indoors; however, the football team assembled on the field for its usual practice.

> The south wing of the men's dorm was completed in August; the new field house should be ready by next fall.

Commas are generally used to separate sentence elements in a series.

> The teacher insisted that we listen closely, write the instructions in our notebook, and follow them precisely when we wrote our reference paper.

Note that a comma is inserted before the coordinate conjunction, *and*, that precedes the last element in the series. Following convention, newspaper and magazine writers omit the comma before the last element; however, the *United States Government Printing Office Style Manual* requires the final comma. Students in college English courses are usually instructed to insert the comma before the last element in a series.

For the sake of variety—or for some more specific reason—writers sometimes omit the conjunction before the last element in the series.

> At Kentucky Lake we spent most of the day boating, fishing, swimming.

The semicolon (rather than the comma) is sometimes used to separate items in a series if they are unusually long or internally punctuated.

> Several solutions have been suggested to alleviate the problem: bringing water in by tank truck; drilling for additional wells, which seems impractical; and asking the people to use water only when absolutely necessary.

EXERCISE 59

Read the following statements carefully and insert the punctuation that is needed. To the left of the statement, indicate by number the principle you applied.

1. Comma or Semicolon Between Independent Clauses
2. Commas or Semicolons Between Items in a Series
3. Correct

_____ 1. My favorite sports are basketball baseball and tennis.

_____ 2. The sundrenched grass was brown from lack of rain the weather man promised no relief from the drought.

_____ 3. His lunch usually consisted of a sandwich and a glass of milk.

_____ 4. I talked with the personnel director filled out the application form and took a series of tests.

_____ 5. The press radio and television have warned the citizens of the dangers of fire because of the drought.

_____ 6. The booklet gave clear instructions on how the power mower should be assembled the quantity and type of lubricants that should be used and the periodic maintenance that should be employed to keep the mower in perfect running order.

_____ 7. One battleship, two cruisers, and six destroyers made up the task force.

_____ 8. We left Birmingham at eight in the morning we reached New Orleans at four that afternoon.

_____ 9. We left our seats walked under the grandstand and bought hot dogs and coffee.

_____ 10. His academic adviser told him that he should take the remedial English course that he should spend at least four hours a day in outside study that he should not participate in extracurricular activities during his freshman year.

_____ 11. The Delta Queen docked at the foot of Fourth Street in Louisville for several hours then it got underway for Evansville.

_____ 12. Donald Carl and Earl decided to make the trip together.

_____ 13. Hunting and fishing and swimming are my favorite outdoor sports.

_____ 14. The plane for Memphis Dallas and Los Angeles taxied to the end of the runway.

_____ 15. Tom stopped by the grocery and bought a quart of milk a loaf of bread and a pound of bologna.

EXERCISE 60

Read the following statements carefully and insert the punctuation that is needed. To the left of the statement, indicate by number the principle you applied.

1. Comma or Semicolon Between Independent Clauses
2. Commas or Semicolons Between Items in a Series
3. Correct

_____ 1. Joe stopped by the bookstore and bought a red pencil and a shorthand notebook.

_____ 2. The paint on the house was chipping and peeling but the owners could not afford to have it repainted.

_____ 3. We took our final exams before the Christmas holidays thus we did not have to worry about books until we returned after the first of the year.

_____ 4. To be considered for the fellowship, I was obliged to fill out a number of forms and submit several letters of reference from former teachers.

_____ 5. Karen, Nan and Donna decided to spend the summer in Maine working as waitresses at a hotel.

_____ 6. The band marched to the opposite side of the playing field then they began to play the "Stars and Stripes Forever."

_____ 7. His desk and chair and typewriter were near the window.

_____ 8. We spent most of our vacation walking about the French Quarter and visiting the many points of historical interest.

_____ 9. His doctor told him that he should eat plenty of red meat that he should get plenty of exercise and that he should sleep at least eight hours every night.

_____ 10. He did not make a passing grade in composition on the placement test therefore he was obliged to take remedial English.

_____ 11. When he came home from work, he took off his shoes sat in his easy chair and began to read his newspaper.

_____ 12. The President, Provost, and Dean were the principal speakers at the freshman convocation.

_____ 13. The students arrived at the stadium by bus in cars and on foot, all keyed up for the homecoming game.

_____ 14. We left the theater and walked over to Broadway, because we were anxious to see Times Square at that time of the evening.

_____ 15. The bus for Springfield St. Louis and Kansas City left on time.

Commas after introductory elements

A comma is generally inserted after introductory elements (clauses or phrases), unless the introductory element is short, in which case the comma may be omitted if the meaning is clear without it.

> Since the Fourth of July was only two days away, the stores were doing a thriving business in fireworks.
>
> On the bus I met one of my former shipmates.

Commas between coordinate adjectives

A comma is inserted between coordinate (equal value) adjectives when the conjunction is omitted.

> The calm, clear water of the river looked inviting.

To determine whether or not the adjectives are coordinate, read the sentence with a conjunction between the words in question. If the construction sounds right (e.g., the calm *and* clear water) the writer can be reasonably sure that the adjectives are coordinate and a comma is needed. On the other hand, if the construction sounds awkward (e.g., the little *and* old lady) the writer can assume that the adjectives *little* and *old* are not coordinate and a comma is not required.

> The teacher had a difficult time controlling the anxious, restless teen-agers.
>
> The scorching midday sun made us move under the trees.

Commas to prevent misreading

A comma is frequently needed for the sake of clarity or to prevent misreading, although no formal rule is applicable. The writer, however, is not only justified but also obliged to use the comma in such instances, for the main purpose of punctuation is to insure clarity and avoid misunderstanding.

> After all, the field trips will help them as much as their classroom work.
>
> High above, the mountain looked as if it were holding up the sky.

EXERCISE 61

Read the following statements carefully and insert the punctuation that is needed. To the left of the statement, indicate by number the principle you applied.

1. After Introductory Elements
2. Between Coordinate Adjectives
3. To Prevent Misreading
4. Correct

_____ 1. When I returned Tom had finished writing the letter.

_____ 2. Having two hours between trains we decided to take a quick tour of the French Quarter.

_____ 3. Although some of the students were weak in fundamentals they were all eager to learn.

_____ 4. David answered in a harsh bitter tone that betrayed his seething hostility.

_____ 5. A large gray squirrel scampered toward the tree.

_____ 6. Leaving the air conditioned library we felt as if we were entering a furnace.

_____ 7. After all the painstaking effort he devoted to the survey produced new insights into the problem.

_____ 8. His scintillating personality caused him to be well liked by his students.

_____ 9. Having received a summons from the Dean of Studies Reed walked gloomily toward the Administration Building.

_____ 10. His ancient battered Ford was festooned with purple and gold streamers.

_____ 11. For many a college or university is merely a country club for social activities.

_____ 12. An hour later a second-class boatswain's mate appeared to march us to our permanent barracks.

_____ 13. Although I could not go to Birmingham for the game I listened to it on the radio.

_____ 14. The shouting pushing crowd gathered before the American Embassy.

_____ 15. Above the colorful Japanese lanterns stretched across the dance floor.

_____ 16. The bright crisp day was perfect for football.

_____ 17. Because Joan could not stand the smoke we had to leave the dance.

_____ 18. Outside the rain continued to fall in gusty torrents.

_____ 19. Although he presented his proposal before the City Council he did not succeed in getting it accepted.

_____ 20. The light having changed to green we continued down Fifth Avenue.

EXERCISE 62

Read the following statements carefully and insert the punctuation that is needed. To the left of the statement, indicate by number the principle you applied.

1. After Introductory Elements
2. Between Coordinate Adjectives
3. To Prevent Misreading
4. Correct

_____ 1. Tying our horses to a tree we climbed down the cliff and walked to the river bank.

_____ 2. After all my efforts did help us to get a brief extension on our leaves.

_____ 3. The cheerful courteous porter helped the lady with her luggage.

_____ 4. Although I did not have time to drive all the way to Florida during the spring vacation I was able to get to New York for several days.

_____ 5. Above the helicopter hovered over the airport waiting for landing instructions.

_____ 6. The screaming hysterical crowd rushed onto the field after the game and almost mobbed the players.

_____ 7. Having received a notice that his insurance was overdue Erwin immediately wrote a check, put it into the self-addressed envelope, and took it to the post office.

_____ 8. Keith sang the song in a deep mellow voice that greatly pleased the audience.

_____ 9. The jaunty old man took us on a tour of the historical church.

_____ 10. If I do not get a raise next month I am going to try to find another job.

_____ 11. Outside the nurse and the doctor spoke frankly about his chances of recovery.

_____ 12. Since I do not intend to return to school next year I am not too worried about the final exams.

_____ 13. His old battered hat was a startling contrast to his rented tuxedo.

_____ 14. Grading themes and preparing lectures consumed much of his free time.

_____ 15. Although some of the students made superior scores on the placement test all were required to take the basic English course.

_____ 16. The policeman having waved his arm to continue we did not stop for the red light.

_____ 17. For some time is a commodity to waste in senseless activity.

_____ 18. Since we did not have a Saturday class we decided to go home for the weekend.

_____ 19. Having received a high grade on all my tests I was not required to take a final exam.

_____ 20. When I returned my uncle's car was parked in front of the house.

Restrictive and nonrestrictive modifiers

Restrictive (essential) modifiers are *not* set off by commas, but nonrestrictive (unnecessary) modifiers *are* set off by commas. A restrictive modifier is essential to convey the main idea in a sentence.

The man *who is standing near the door* is my uncle.

Who is standing near the door is a functional part of the sentence. If the clause were deleted the meaning of the sentence would be changed. Hence restrictive modifiers are not enclosed by commas, dashes, or parentheses.

A nonrestrictive modifier, although adding important information, is not absolutely necessary to the main idea of the sentence.

My Uncle George, who used to be a stockbroker, now lives in Florida.

Nonrestrictive (or nonessential) modifiers are generally set off by commas. But if the modifiers are internally punctuated or cause an abrupt break in the rhythm of the sentence, they are usually set off by dashes or parentheses.

I was instructed to place my clothes in a cardboard box, which was later shipped home.

Three boats—one with an outboard and two with inboard motors—were tied to the same dock.

The two coaches (one was wearing a sport shirt) rushed onto the field to help the injured player.

EXERCISE 63

The following sentences contain modifiers that are either restrictive (essential) or nonrestrictive (nonessential). Insert the needed punctuation—commas, dashes, or parentheses—if the modifier is nonrestrictive. To the left, indicate the classification by writing *R* for restrictive or *N* for nonrestrictive.

_____ 1. Our Federal marshal who had been a first sergeant in World War II displayed great courage in apprehending the escaped convicts.

_____ 2. Three players the center, the fullback, and the left end carried the quarterback off the field.

_____ 3. Novels that enabled us to get deeper insights into life were recommended by our literature teacher.

_____ 4. The elderly gentleman who took our tickets is the assistant principal.

_____ 5. The girl wearing the light green sweater will probably win the first prize.

_____ 6. The president of the First National Bank who has been one of our leading citizens for years was elected chairman of the Heart Fund Drive.

_____ 7. The jury made up of citizens of the county seat listened to the summation of the prosecuting attorney.

_____ 8. The actor whom I greatly admire received the Academy Award for his supporting role.

_____ 9. Dr. Reid having finished the operation took off his gloves.

_____ 10. Three officers a captain and two lieutenants inspected the barracks.

_____ 11. The person who arrives first should kindle the fire.

_____ 12. Mr. Hughes who is a dynamic speaker gave the welcoming address to the freshmen.

_____ 13. Mr. Krupp whom I consider my best teacher coached the football team.

_____ 14. Many novels that become best sellers have no great literary value.

_____ 15. The gossip column which is usually amusing was read first by most of the students.

_____ 16. The man in the blue suit is my father.

_____ 17. The three bands two from the local high schools and the other from the university assembled at the end of the field.

_____ 18. The quarterback who happens to be my classmate threw two touchdown passes.

_____ 19. The water tower that you see when you enter town is no longer used.

_____ 20. The two horses one black and the other chestnut snorted and kicked angrily in their stalls.

EXERCISE 64

The sentences below contain modifiers that are either restrictive (essential) or nonrestrictive (nonessential). Insert the needed punctuation—commas, dashes, or parentheses—if the modifier is nonrestrictive. To the left, indicate the classification by writing *R* for restrictive or *N* for nonrestrictive.

_____ 1. The wooded area that you see in the distance is part of the state forest reserve.

_____ 2. Three school buses all of them painted yellow were parked in front of the school.

_____ 3. The two horses in the inside post positions both of them three-year-olds are favored to win the race.

_____ 4. The player who I thought was outstanding did not receive the most valuable player award.

_____ 5. The narcotics agent having investigated the drug store burglary returned to his office to write the case report.

_____ 6. The three executives the president, vice-president, and secretary decided to close the plant for repairs.

_____ 7. Poems that seem to be pointless usually hold no interest for the students.

_____ 8. The president of the university who had been a general in World War II delivered the welcoming address.

_____ 9. The policeman who gave me the ticket has a reputation for being a sadist.

_____ 10. The Secretary of State who was dressed formally for the occasion shook hands with the King and Queen as they reached the end of the gangplank.

_____ 11. The priest who celebrated the Mass is the pastor of our church.

_____ 12. Many grammatical rules that confuse the students should be eliminated from freshman textbooks.

_____ 13. Rev. Carlson who formerly was a chaplain in the Navy delivered the keynote address.

_____ 14. Senator Smith whom I consider eminently qualified spoke on the dangers of our present foreign policy.

_____ 15. The students who average 90% on their monthly reports do not have to take the final exams.

_____ 16. Three officials from the Board of Health a physician, a nurse, and an administrator inspected the field hospital.

_____ 17. The judge who was finally picked to preside over the trial was recruited from a county at the far end of the state.

_____ 18. The chairman of the board who presented the safety awards was formerly president of the firm.

_____ 19. The man in the blue overalls was hired to trim the trees.

_____ 20. The short stories of James Joyce which often do not appeal to college freshmen are usually based on incidents from real life.

Other uses of commas, dashes, and parentheses

Elements out of position Commas—and sometimes dashes and parentheses—are used to set off elements that are moved from their usual position in the sentence.

> The game, I am afraid, will be postponed because of wet grounds.
>
> The game—if I may hazard a guess—will probably be a free-scoring affair.
>
> The meaning of the story (I believe most of you will agree) is not perfectly clear.

Introductory adverbs and interrupters within the sentence A comma is generally placed after connective adverbs that are used at the beginning of a sentence or an independent clause.

> However, I am convinced that he was to blame for the accident.

Commas are used to set off adverbs and other interrupters when they are used within the sentence.

> I believe, however, that he should be given another chance.
>
> Collecting stamps, as a matter of fact, is also my hobby.

Appositives Commas (and sometimes dashes and parentheses) are used to set off appositives—nouns or noun substitutes set next to other nouns or noun substitutes which they rename.

> The fantail, the aftermost part of the ship, was hardly visible because of the high waves.
>
> Mr. Jones—my best high school teacher—was a graduate of Indiana University.
>
> Both senators from my home state (Louis Traud and John Duggers) were present for the official opening of the bridge.

Direct Address Commas are used to set off proper names or titles used in direct address.

> Call me, Harry, as soon as you reach Cincinnati.
>
> I feel confident, Senator, that the subsidy bill will eventually be enacted.

Mild Interjections A comma is used after mild interjections.

> No, I would rather not go to the play.
>
> Yes, I will be there at eight.

EXERCISE 65

Read the following sentences carefully and insert the punctuation that is needed. In the left-hand column, indicate by number the rule you applied.

1. Introductory Connective or Interrupter
2. Element Out of Position
3. Appositive
4. Direct Address
5. Mild Interjection

_____ 1. Joe how about playing tennis this afternoon?

_____ 2. I doubt however that the farm subsidy bill will be enacted.

_____ 3. Joan do you want another sandwich?

_____ 4. This summer if I am still living I plan to spend two weeks at Cape Cod.

_____ 5. Mr. Hyde a former FBI agent related to us some of his exciting experiences.

_____ 6. Yes it is a magnificent symphony.

_____ 7. He has a definite advantage of course because of his weight.

_____ 8. I feel confident Mr. Hunt that I can do the work satisfactorily.

_____ 9. I hold fast therefore to my opinion that the dismissal of the board chairman was not justified.

_____ 10. No I would rather go to the movies.

_____ 11. The rampaging river I believe has reached its crest.

_____ 12. The girls spent the entire afternoon at the sorority house scrubbing, sweeping, dusting in preparation for the tea.

_____ 13. Joseph Dugan our Police Chief attended the FBI Academy in Washington.

_____ 14. Arguing with a traffic cop I had to admit was the best way to get a ticket.

_____ 15. His ironical statements deliberate misinterpretations were baffling to some of the students.

EXERCISE 66

Read the following sentences carefully and insert the punctuation that is needed. In the left-hand column, indicate by number the rule you applied.

1. Introductory Connective or Interrupter
2. Element Out of Position
3. Appositive
4. Direct Address
5. Mild Interjection

_____ 1. Tom what route do you think we should take on our return trip?

_____ 2. I am not convinced though that the old post office should be replaced.

_____ 3. Ted do you think I would be better off buying a new car or having the old one repaired?

_____ 4. This summer if I can get my parents' permission I plan to spend several weeks in France.

_____ 5. Dr. Garrison a former medical officer in the U.S. Navy told us of some of his experiences on Guam during World War II.

_____ 6. No I am afraid I will not be able to go on the field trip next Saturday.

_____ 7. It is not perfectly clear for instance why he left school and returned to New York without informing his parents.

_____ 8. I am reasonably sure Mr. Jesse that I can meet you Friday morning in Cincinnati for the interview.

_____ 9. We can safely conclude therefore that the accident would have never happened if the prescribed rules had been observed.

_____ 10. Yes I will be delighted to attend the meeting.

_____ 11. The most difficult part of the examination I believe has been completed.

_____ 12. The mob of angry students the newspaper reported gathered in front of the administration building to protest the new curfew regulation.

_____ 13. Bob Morris the master of ceremonies at the banquet has a sparkling personality and a warm sense of humor.

_____ 14. Turning in a sloppy paper I am now convinced is one sure way of getting an F.

_____ 15. The use of irony in an essay or story saying the opposite of what one really means is rather dangerous; for many readers do not comprehend the intention of the author.

Quotation Marks

Double quotation marks ("...") are used to enclose the exact words of another writer or a speaker in dialogue.

> In the *Preface to a Dictionary of the English Language,* Samuel Johnson describes how he approached this mammoth project: "Having therefore no assistance but from general grammar, I applied myself to the perusal of our writers...."

The use of double quotation marks ("...") is the usual way of indicating the exact words of another writer or the speech of a character in a story. However, a second technique, used for longer quotes, is considered standard procedure in writing college reference or term papers. If the quotation is more than five lines, the material is block indented and single spaced; no quotation marks are used. Paragraphs are indented three spaces rather than the customary five.

In the *Preface to a Dictionary of the English Language,* Samuel Johnson describes how he approached this mammoth project.

> Having therefore no assistance but from general grammar, I applied myself to the perusal of our writers; and noting whatever might be of use to ascertain or illustrate any word or phrase, accumulated in time the materials of a dictionary, which, by degrees, I reduced to method, establishing to myself, in the progress of the work, such rules as experience and analogy suggested to me ....

In using quotation marks to enclose the exact words of the speaker in dialogue, most professional writers begin a new paragraph for each new speaker.

> "Cold," the old man answered blowing on his chapped hands. "That wind's like a knife. You better give me a cup of hot chocolate to warm me up."
> Carl smiled and drew a glass of beer and set it on the bar in front of him.
> A sly look appeared on the old man's face. "Say, Carl, you made a mistake. I wanted hot chocolate. Well, as long as you got it drawn I won't let it go to waste."
> "I'm certainly sorry," Carl apologized. "I could have sworn that was hot chocolate."

Double quotation marks are also used to enclose the following:

TITLES OF SHORT STORIES
> "Counterparts" from *Dubliners* by James Joyce is one of my favorite short stories.

POEMS NOT PUBLISHED AS A SEPARATE VOLUME
> "Woman's Constancy" is one of John Donne's earlier poems.

ARTICLES FROM MAGAZINES
> "The Danger of Education in America," an article in this week's *Life,* is worth reading.

> The introductory chapter, "The Substance of Shakespearean Tragedy" from *Shakespearean Tragedy* by A. C. Bradley, is profound without being pedantic.

Single quotation marks ('. . .') are used to enclose a quotation within a quotation.

> John crumbled up the latest issue of the college newspaper and vehemently threw it into the wastepaper basket. "This new curfew rule is for the birds. 'Give me liberty or give me death.' "

Note that the period goes inside the single quotation mark.

Confusion sometimes arises when quotation marks and other punctuation fall together. Periods and commas go inside single and double quotation marks.

> Dr. Moore said, "Your term papers are due the first Monday of the last week of the semester."
>
> "I believe," he said, "that every student (unless he is physically handicapped) should be a member of one of the teams."

Colons and semicolons go outside the quotation marks.

> Dr. Mason said, "Each color of the flag has a definite symbolic meaning": red, white, and blue.
>
> Dr. Kesler concluded, "Thus you can see the close connection between psychology and literature"; then he walked out of the classroom.

Dashes to indicate an abrupt stop or an unfinished speech go inside the quotation marks.

> "And I further promise that if I am elected—" with that, somebody in the audience threw a tomato.

The question mark and exclamation point go inside or outside, depending on whether the entire statement or only the quoted material is a question or exclamation. If only the quoted part of the sentence is a question or exclamation, the punctuation goes inside the quotation marks. Otherwise it goes outside.

> Did he say, "Only the seniors can go on the trip"?
>
> The principal entered the room and asked, "How many of you expect to go on the trip?"
>
> Oh, how I enjoyed Poe's poem "The Raven"!
>
> He stuck his head out the window and shouted, "Come back here you dirty bum!"

EXERCISE 67

Correctly punctuate the following statements by inserting the proper marks and by circling the ones that are misused.

1. Did he say that "term papers were due Monday?"

2. Whitman's famous poem O Captain! My Captain was written to lament the death of Lincoln.

3. Dr. Durham said, "I have to be in Chicago Saturday night;" therefore, he will not be able to come to the dance.

4. Did he say, "Everyone on the team will make the trip?"

5. My Father said to me, "I am glad that you decided to go to college".

6. He replied by citing the following quotation from Emerson: "The President pays dearly for his White House".

7. "Don't go into the deep water unless you can swim across the pool " the lifeguard shouted!

8. Dr. Fowler said that "he would try his best to come to the dance Saturday night."

9. The sergeant walked into the barracks and shouted, "Everyone outside for muster"!

10. "Come down out of that tree," his father shouted from the back porch!

11. "The boat trip along the Mississippi, John said, "was educational."

12. "What business is it of yours," he asked sarcastically?

13. The Life of Faith is the concluding chapter of Paul Tillich's stimulating book, *Dynamics of Faith.*

14. "I suppose," he said, "a little frustration now and then never killed anyone. 'Sweet are the uses of adversity'."

15. She concluded her remarks by reminding the class, "*You* are your best teacher".

EXERCISE 68

Correctly punctuate the following statements by inserting the proper marks and by circling the ones that are misused.

1. Dr. Johnson said, "I'm sorry, but I won't be able to make it Saturday night;" so we asked Dr. Egan to oversee the dance.

2. "Let's take my car", he insisted.

3. Adventure is one of the more memorable stories from *Winesburg, Ohio* by Sherwood Anderson.

4. "To the rear march," the drill sergeant shouted loudly!

5. "What time do you want me to meet you," he asked?

6. "Neither a borrower nor a lender be, Polonius advised his son, "for loan oft loses both self and friend."

7. When he drove me to the airport he said, "Let me know what you think of the samples".

8. Vice, Crime and Marijuana, a penetrating article by Rodney Gilbert, appeared in the March 1963 edition of *Legion.*

9. "The most difficult part of the operation," the sergeant said, is to capture the sentries at both ends of the bridge ".

10. "I am a little puzzled," he said, "about the meaning of Hemingway's novel *For Whom the Bell Tolls.* Although Hemingway takes the title for his novel from John Donne's essay, he seems to contradict Donne's belief that 'God is our only security ' ".

11. "Is it true," he asked, that Russian students even in the lower grades study English?

12. "I promise if I am elected everyone will have a steady job and . . ." he droned on endlessly.

13. The poem Chicago by Carl Sandburg is frequently quoted.

14. John said that "he enjoyed his visit to the zoo."

15. The Knight's Tale is the first of the stories in *The Canterbury Tales* by Geoffrey Chaucer.

Apostrophes

The apostrophe (') is used with nouns or pronouns to indicate possession.

> *John's* bicycle was stolen.
> The *Smiths'* car has a flat tire.
> *One's* success often hinges on having a college education.

Singular nouns that do not end in *s* form their possessive by adding *'s*.

boy	boy's
girl	girl's
tooth	tooth's
mouse	mouse's

Singular nouns that end in *s* form their possessives by adding either an apostrophe after the *s* (James') or an apostrophe and an *s* (James's). If the additional *s* makes an awkward pronunciation, use only the apostrophe.

> Xerxes' army
> Moses' followers
> Keats' poems

Plural nouns that do not end in *s* form their possessives by adding an apostrophe and an *s*.

men's	teeth's
women's	mice's
oxen's	

Plural nouns that end in *s* form their possessives by adding only the apostrophe.

babies'	boys'
fathers'	dogs'
soldiers'	brothers'
schoolgirls'	horses'

The possessive case of hyphenated words is formed by adding the apostrophe and *s* to the final word.

> My brother-in-law's car
> My brothers-in-law's cars

If joint possession is to be shown, only the last noun is in the possessive case.

> John and Robert's boat
> (They own the boat together.)
>
> Helen's and Joan's books
> (They own the books separately.)

Apostrophes are not used with personal possessive pronouns (*his, hers, ours, theirs, yours, its*) or the relative interrogative pronoun (*whose*).

His coat is on the bed.

That painting is *hers.*

The boat at the end of the dock is *ours.*

Does this book happen to be *yours?*

Whose car is parked in front of the house?

The following possessives and contractions are frequently confused in student writing. Often students write *who's* when they mean *whose* and *you're* when they mean *your* and *they're* when they mean *their* and *it's* when they mean *its.* If you will remember that the hyphenated forms are a contraction of a pronoun and verb (*who's* is equivalent to *who is* and *you're* is equivalent to *you are*) and the unhyphenated words show possession, you should have no trouble in choosing the correct form.

Who's coming to the party?	*They're* sure they can be there.
Whose record player is that?	*Their* reaction was predictable.
You're the one I've been looking for.	*It's* too late to catch the train.
Your car has a flat tire.	*Its* sudden bark frightened me.

The possessive of indefinite pronouns is formed by adding an apostrophe and *s* to the singular.

anybody's business	one's personality
anyone's opinion	nobody's concern
everybody's belief	someone's mistake

Apostrophes are used to mark the omission of letters in contracted words or figures in dates.

cannot	can't	I have	I've
I am	I'm	has not	hasn't
I will	I'll	is not	isn't
it is	it's	1949	'49

Apostrophes are used in dialectal speech to mark the omission of one or more letters in a word.

I'm *goin'* downtown.

Give me a *duz'n* eggs.

An apostrophe and *s* are used to form the plural of letters and figures and words used as words.

Be sure to dot your *i*'s and cross your *t*'s.

His *6*'s look like *8*'s.

He has ten *and*'s in the first two sentences.

The apostrophe and *s* are used with some idiomatic expressions.

This *month's* quota is larger than the previous *month's.*

An *hour's* walk brought us to the lake.

I reached my *wits'* end before he told me the answer.

EXERCISE 69

Insert the punctuation that is needed and circle the punctuation that is misused.

1. My sister's-in-law hat took the prize in the Easter Parade.
2. Xerxes army won an overwhelming victory.
3. Its too bad that he didn't win the first prize.
4. The two cars parked in front of the fraternity house are our's.
5. The mouses tail was caught in the trap.
6. Whose going to pay the travel expenses when the debating team goes to Chicago?
7. His 4s look like 7s.
8. Ones political beliefs are often shaped by parental influences.
9. The dogs tails wagged as we approached the house.
10. My mother's-in-law biscuits are delicious.
11. James car was parked in front of his house.
12. Tom's and Harry's horse won the fifth race.
13. Anyones opinion is valid if it is logical and supported by facts.
14. My brothers wives had their annual reunion.
15. Everybodys beliefs should be respected.
16. The boys jackets were all the same color.
17. Dick and Jim's books were on the desks.
18. The soldiers shoes were highly polished.
19. The class of 33 had it's annual reunion.
20. Its going to rain.

EXERCISE 70

Insert the punctuation that is needed and circle the punctuation that is misused.

1. How many *l*'s and how many *t*-s are in his name?
2. I am sure that the themes he read in class were their's.
3. Whether or not to accept the job is nobodys concern but his.
4. I was sure that the poem he read was your's.
5. The mens uniforms were neatly pressed.
6. My brothers-in-law boyhood homes were in the same block.
7. The oxens flanks shimmered in the midday sun.
8. The boy's clothes were soaked by the rain.
9. Its an ideal day for football.
10. The eagle dived on it's prey; then soared into the air.
11. Jack and Ted's guns were on the shelf.
12. Someones mistake fouled up the whole process.
13. Who's girl friend do you think will be chosen queen?
14. He seemed to be imbued with the spirit of 76.
15. Mary and Jane's coats were hanging in the closet.
16. Keats poems were discussed by the class.
17. Its a misdemeanor to hunt without a license.
18. The document bristled with *hence*-s and *so*-s.
19. Moses followers roamed for forty years before they reached the Promised Land.
20. The horses bridles were hanging in front of the stalls.

Parentheses

Punctuation marks called parentheses ( ) are used within a sentence to enclose a qualifying comment or an explanation that may add to the meaning but that is unessential to the grammatical structure of the sentence. Moreover, a complete sentence or several sentences may be considered parenthetical. In such a case parentheses are placed before the first word and after the final period, as in the third example that follows:

> The United Nations Organization (established after the hostilities in World War II came to an end) has made substantial progress toward world peace.

> Dugan's grandfather (an Irish immigrant) was one of the original settlers of New Dublin, Ohio.

> From daybreak to sundown the planes took off and landed on the aircraft carrier. (I will say more about this operation later.)

Parentheses are generally used to enclose letters or numbers that precede a listing.

> The officer gave me the following instructions before I caught the train for Chicago: (1) eat breakfast at the train station when you arrive in Chicago, (2) board the Northshore train at Wabash Avenue Station, (3) report to the receiving center at Great Lakes, (4) have the officer-of-the-day sign the sealed orders.

Parentheses are sometimes used to clarify an ambiguous pronoun reference.

> John told his father that his (John's) car had been wrecked.

Parentheses are used to enclose cross references.

> The faculty have published articles in fifteen learned journals. (See Appendix A for detailed listing.)

In some formal writing, parentheses are used to restate numbers and amounts that are spelled out in the document.

> The convention was attended by seventy-five (75) bishops and priests.

> The undersigned promises to pay four hundred dollars ($400) six months from the date of this note.

Brackets

Brackets [ ] do not appear on the keyboard of standard typewriters but are made with the slant and the underscore keys. They are used to enclose explanatory material or editorial comments within a passage, especially a quoted passage.

> "Amen I say to you, no prophet [this certainly applied to Jesus] is acceptable in his own country."

Brackets are used to enclose the Latin word *sic* (which means *thus*) to indicate that the preceding word or phrase is written exactly as it appeared in the original text.

> The students should be seperated [*sic*] according to their abilities.

Italics

In typewritten or longhand papers, italics are indicated by underlining.

Critics are generally agreed that Paradise Lost is Milton's magnum opus.

In a typewritten or handwritten manuscript, the following items should be underlined.

Names of magazines and newspapers	The New York Times Newsweek Saturday Evening Post
Titles of books, motion pictures, works of art, names of ships and planes	The Old Man and the Sea El Cid The Thinker Queen Mary Spirit of St. Louis
The titles of plays and other literary works published separately	J.B. Othello Paradise Lost

Foreign words that are not considered standard English   After his scathing editorial in the Torch, he was persona non grata among his teachers.

Sirloin steak was the pièce de résistance of the meal.

Underline to call particular attention to the word or letter or figure being named. (Sometimes quotes are used.)

What does dubiously mean?
Don't forget to dot your i's and cross your t's.
I could not tell if the last figure was 5 or 7.

Shorter literary works (short stories, essays, and poems) that are published in a volume or anthology are enclosed by quotation marks rather than underlined.

"The Boarding House" from Dubliners by James Joyce
"Birth of Christ" from The Life of the Virgin Mary by Rainer Maria Rilke

Dashes

The dash (two unspaced hyphens if written on a typewriter) is a flexible and useful punctuation mark if used correctly. When used haphazardly, it connotes carelessness and ignorance and implies that the writer lacks even a rudimentary understanding of punctuation.

The dash is used to indicate an abrupt break in the continuity of a sentence

On my first trip to Trinidad—I'll tell you about that later.

He told us they discovered gold—who could believe such a story?—on their first expedition.

or to emphasize a word or phrase at the end of a sentence.

> Thomas Wolfe admitted that he had only one goal in life—fame.
>
> Roosevelt had one consuming ambition—to be President of the United States.

The dash is also used in place of a colon before a listing or summary in less formal writing

> He had the qualities of a great leader—courage, humility, and fairness.
>
> The ability to hold the attention of the class, the imagination to allow for individual differences, the restraint and humor to control his emotions—these are some of the qualities of an effective teacher.

and to set off abrupt parenthetical elements or elements that are internally punctuated.

> I would like to tell you—if I may be so presumptuous—what is wrong with our educational system.
>
> Four ships—two destroyers, a cruiser, and an aircraft carrier—were anchored within sight of Puerto Rico.

EXERCISE 71

Draw a circle around the incorrect punctuation and insert the correct punctuation as needed.

1. If I'm able to save enough money to . . . there I go dreaming again.

2. All of the board members have distinguished themselves in academic affairs. See Appendix A.

3. The plane in which Lindberg flew the Atlantic (the "Spirit of St. Louis") is on display in a Washington museum.

4. George told Bob that he, Bob, forgot to turn off his headlights.

5. "Your answer is *to* (*sic*) short."

6. Be sure to take the following precautions: 1 boil the drinking water; 2 be extremely careful to put out all fires; 3 do not fish off the dam.

7. I am quite certain, unless something extraordinary happens, that I can attend the meeting.

8. The 6 percent -6%- interest is due six months from date.

9. New Orleans is called the Crescent City. (Evansville is also called the Crescent City).

10. "The Wall Street Journal" contains the latest published reports on the stock market.

11. The department is authorized to have two -2- professors, three -3- associate professors, four -4- assistant professors, and six -6- instructors.

12. A group of students, mostly boys, congregated in front of the Student Union Building.

13. He read "Time" and "Newsweek," trying to detect if the news reports had been slanted.

14. The Golden Gate Press has recently published an excellent edition of "Hamlet."

15. That was a fetching "fraulein" you had a date with last night.

16. Iago's feelings with respect to Othello are stated early in the play: "Though I do hate him as I do Hell pains (a figure of speech that would suggest that Iago is not without religious beliefs), yet for necessity of present life I must show out a flag and sign of love."

17. Our trip to Lincoln's birthplace, about thirty miles from Louisville, was the high point of our trip.

18. The surgical supplies, a scalpel, clamps, and bandages, were arranged on the table next to the bed.

19. A reproduction of Rodin's "The Thinker" has been placed in front of the Administration Building.

20. What does "propaganda" mean in this instance?

EXERCISE 72

Draw a circle around the incorrect punctuation and insert the correct punctuation as needed.

1. Fifteen persons have served as president of Holiday Swim Club. See listing attached.

2. If we act now we will be able to purchase the lot for two thousand dollars [$2,000].

3. The "Queen Mary" is scheduled to dock at 5:00 P.M.

4. Three soldiers, two privates and a corporal, were cutting the grass around the barracks.

5. The short story of Kafka entitled *The Country Doctor* was the most difficult one in the anthology to understand.

6. "Hasta mañana," he shouted as he rushed out the door.

7. The Council shall consist of twelve —12— members.

8. "The prologue to Chaucer's *Canterbury Tales* begins on an idyllic note: "Whan that Aprille with his shoures sote (When April with his showers sweet)"

9. The two jockeys [one in green silks and the other in red] walked toward the scales.

10. "If he doesn't give me a raise . . ." Logan was off on one of his wild stories.

11. His writing is hard to read because his "e's" look like "l's."

12. I thought that "El Cid" was a better movie than "Ben Hur."

13. Some critics feel that "The Sound and the Fury" is Faulkner's greatest novel.

14. Nancy told her sister that her—Nancy's—boyfriend was downstairs.

15. We used a paperbacked copy of "King Lear" in our literature course.

16. My uncle from Cincinnati, the one who owns the race horses, drove down for the Derby.

17. He was an avid reader of the "Saturday Review of Literature."

18. Three cars, a Buick, a Rambler, and a Ford, were side by side waiting for the traffic light to turn green.

19. He enjoyed reading the "Christian Science Monitor."

20. "I have not been *effected* (*sic*) by your decision."

EXERCISE 73 / General review of punctuation

The sentences that follow are either correct or contain one or more punctuation errors. Circle the punctuation that is incorrect and insert the correct punctuation as needed. If the sentence is correct put a *C* to the left of the number.

_____ 1. He asked me if I knew the best route to New York?

_____ 2. We left New York around noon we arrived in Boston five hours later.

_____ 3. Tom and Harry's cameras were imported from Germany.

_____ 4. Don Jarett our football coach graduated from Northwestern University.

_____ 5. The boys caps were of the same color and design.

_____ 6. Do you think there may be organic life on Mars.

_____ 7. The following students from our class made the honor roll. Begley, Raburn, and Nichols.

_____ 8. The first building you pass when you approach our town from the east is the County High School.

_____ 9. For many the opportunity to attend college is considered a right rather than a privilege.

_____ 10. In my opinion "The New York Times" is the best newspaper in the United States.

_____ 11. The camping supplies, a tent, cooking utensils, and bedding, were packed carefully in my car.

_____ 12. "The Sun Also Rises" was the first of Hemingway's novels to be published.

_____ 13. For many years the Grand Ole Opry has been broadcast from Nashville over radio station W.S.M.

_____ 14. The University Press has recently published an excellent edition of "King Lear."

_____ 15. The seething pulsating crowd jammed the bus station.

_____ 16. The person who finishes last will have to buy the drinks.

_____ 17. The magazine section which is usually entertaining is probably read by more people than the editorial page.

_____ 18. The word separate is frequently misspelled.

_____ 19. Dan's and Susan's Restaurant specializes in barbecued ribs.

_____ 20. _Snake_ by William Saroyan from "The Daring Young Man on the Flying Trapeze and Other Short Stories" appeared in our freshman anthology.

_____ 21. The class of 58 was the last to graduate from the old school building.

_____ 22. I believe its going to snow.

_____ 23. He asked me if I planned on working toward a Master's degree?

_____ 24. My sisters husbands came from different parts of the country.

_____ 25. The first island we visited on our Caribbean cruise was Jamaica the next morning we got underway for Trinidad.

_____ 26. "The Coronation of the Virgin" by Velásquez is on display in the Prado, Madrid.

_____ 27. Our entire graduating class, would you believe such a thing, enrolled in colleges and universities.

_____ 28. The soldiers barracks were ready for inspection.

_____ 29. Dr. Adams who is the most popular teacher on the faculty gave the commencement address.

_____ 30. Dr Mason, the Dean of Men, was the first person I met when I reached the campus.

_____ 31. My stay in Mexico, it was only for a few days, was the highlight of the long trip.

_____ 32. Outside the wind caused the leaves to race along the street like frightened animals.

_____ 33. What does sophistication mean in this instance.

_____ 34. *Polaris Sub Prowls the Sea,* an article by Robert Brigham, appeared in the March 22, 1963, edition of "Life".

_____ 35. His battered greasy hat was set at a rakish angle on his head.

_____ 36. Everybodys opinions should be considered carefully.

_____ 37. "What time do you think we should leave," Tom asked his brother?

_____ 38. Ronald and Cecil pooled their money and bought an old Model A Ford.

_____ 39. Above the fleecy clouds drifted across the blue enameled sky.

_____ 40. My plane is supposed to arrive at 3 30 P.M.

_____ 41. I am "muy simpatico" about the whole proposal.

_____ 42. Examinations for the Winter Quarter will begin on Feb 20.

_____ 43. Yes I will definitely attend the convention next month.

_____ 44. I am not at all confident Dr. Hoyer that the manuscript will be ready by the end of the week.

_____ 45. Many stories and essays that are intelligent and well written never get published.

_____ 46. "Who wants to buy an extra ticket to the game," he asked when he entered the lounge?

_____ 47. The bus ride along the Hudson River, Roy said, "was most enjoyable.

_____ 48. Kentucky Lake I believe is the largest lake of its kind in the world.

_____ 49. The sergeant entered the barracks and shouted, "Get out of those bunks"!

_____ 50. The lady in the blue dress is my mother.

EXERCISE 74 / General review of punctuation

The sentences that follow either are correct or contain one or more punctuation errors. Circle the punctuation that is incorrect and insert the correct punctuation as needed. If the sentence is correct put a *C* to the left of the number.

_____ 1. The F.B.I. sent one of their agents to investigate the car theft.

_____ 2. Did he say, "Everyone on the squad would be given a sweater?"

_____ 3. Having received a ticket for speeding he decided that in the future he would obey the traffic laws.

_____ 4. The traffic situation in New York is impossible. (In fact, it is bad in all large cities).

_____ 5. The 5 percent—5%—interest will be added to your savings account.

_____ 6. "Time" and "Life" are published by the same company.

_____ 7. "To the left flank, march," he shouted in a booming voice!

_____ 8. The contract was signed by R M Wilkinson.

_____ 9. Oh I really don't care one way or the other.

_____ 10. My father's-in-law boat was wrecked in the storm.

_____ 11. Senator Jenkins having finished his speech left the platform and returned to his seat in the chamber.

_____ 12. Movies that appeal to a mature audience are becoming fewer each year.

_____ 13. The elderly lady at the end of the reception line is the principal of our school.

_____ 14. The cats back rose when he saw the dog approach.

_____ 15. Whose going to be the first to volunteer to give a pint of blood.

_____ 16. Tom answered the question in a sharp sarcastic tone that betrayed his impatience.

_____ 17. Having several hours to kill we strolled through Central Park.

_____ 18. He said, "I think I'll go swimming this afternoon".

_____ 19. John would you like to walk over to the Student Union and have a cup of coffee.

_____ 20. I doubt however that the courts will dry out in time for the tennis match.

_____ 21. Next winter if I am still living I plan to spend at least a month in Florida.

_____ 22. One of El Greco's splendid paintings, "Saint Martin and the Beggar," was on display at the museum.

_____ 23. Did he say, "The band will accompany the team to the tournament"?

_____ 24. Eudora Welty's short story, _A Piece of News_, was originally published in "A Curtain of Green and Other Stories."

_____ 25. The Dean's secretary typed a copy of the student's complaint to send to the President. "We cannot study in the dormetory (_sic_) because of the excessive noise."

_____ 26. My favorite operas are: _Carmen_ and _The Barber of Seville_.

_____ 27. Our unit was authorized to have one—1—captain, two—2—lieutenants, four—4—sergeants, six—6—corporals, and fifty—50—privates.

_____ 28. Our baseball coach who also taught physics was an excellent athlete.

_____ 29. "Let's take a stroll through the park", he suggested.

_____ 30. George Martin a former Navy flier now has his own private plane.

_____ 31. Joan said, "I have to study for my final exams;" so she won't be able to leave town this weekend.

_____ 32. The lions roar could be heard when we entered the zoo.

_____ 33. I filled out the employment papers took the medical examination and reported for work the same day.

_____ 34. The tennis courts were soaked by the downpour but the scorching sun dried them within a few hours.

_____ 35. This is the road we take, isn't it.

_____ 36. The following men have guard duty tonight. Harris, Brown, and Spencer.

_____ 37. What do you plan to do this summer.

_____ 38. The plane landed at O'Hare Field at 8 30 P.M.

_____ 39. I am quite certain that unless we have an earthquake I can go to the dance.

_____ 40. His 5s look like 8s.

_____ 41. Three policemen a sergeant and two patrolmen escorted the movie star through the crowd.

_____ 42. The word sophistication has more than one meaning.

_____ 43. Ones personal opinions often detract from the objectivity of his writing.

_____ 44. Joan told Sally that she, Sally, had been chosen to represent the sorority.

_____ 45. When I returned the faucet was still dripping.

_____ 46. James essay won first prize in the contest.

_____ 47. The girl wearing the blue sweater will probably be elected cheer leader.

_____ 48. You should follow these instructions: 1 submit a title page; 2 place your outline next; 3 arrange your footnotes and bibliography at the end of your paper.

_____ 49. Two motorcycle policemen and a fire engine led the parade.

_____ 50. After all the time he spent in the Army helped him to mature emotionally.

Lesson 15

Spelling

Spelling is one of the most serious problems in writing for a more important reason than the appearance of a misspelled word on a sheet of paper. A lack of confidence in spelling may be the underlying reason so many people fear even the thought of writing a letter or theme or report. (Perhaps this is one reason that the American Telephone and Telegraph Company is the bluest of all the blue chip stocks on the New York exchange.) Many people would rather do almost anything than write. Could this dread be for fear that someone will think them ignorant if they misspell a few words? Unfortunately, people do judge our writing on the basis of spelling, frequently using this as the only standard of judgment. No matter how you try to rationalize poor spelling, it is a serious problem not only in your college writing but also in letters and reports you may have to write in your job. You need to become a first-rate speller.

First you should overlearn the three hundred frequently misspelled words that are listed at the end of this section, for these words constitute a large percentage of spelling errors in scholastic and commercial writing. Second you should keep a master list of words *you* misspell, studying not only the correct forms but the incorrect originals. We remember chiefly by association, and, if you will write the correct form of the word one syllable at a time below the incorrect, as in the following examples, draw a circle around the trouble spot, then close your eyes and snap a mental picture of the two words, you will probably never make the same mistake again.

sep	(e)	rate
sep	(A)	rate
com men	(se)	rate
com men	(SU)	rate
in	(tra)	ca cies
in	(TRI)	ca cies
in her	(e)	tance
in her	(I)	tance
phi los	(i)	phy
phi los	(O)	phy

The examples we have given are characteristic of most spelling errors found in themes and reports: (1) most trouble in writing the English language comes from the vowel sounds, and (2) most misspelled words are all right except for one trouble spot.

Another reason for misspelled words is that the writer tries to hurry through the word rather than enunciate it clearly and spell one syllable at a time. Thus many words are misspelled because the writers do not pronounce them correctly, such as the following:

nowadays
accommodate
government
different

People often misspell these words because of careless enunciation. For example, if you pronounce *nowadays* (now-days) you may misspell it *nowdays*. Although proper enunciation and pronunciation are imperative, you must not neglect sight—remembering what the word looks like. The avid reader is usually (though not always) a good speller, because he remembers the appearance of words. He would probably never write *seperate* for *separate*, for he sees *separate* in his mind's eye. The person of limited reading experience, though, might misspell *separate* even though he enunciated carefully and wrote one syllable at a time, for the middle vowel *a* has almost the same sound as short *e*. You can realize, then, that the eyes and the mind's ear must work together to gain precision in spelling.

Another way to improve your spelling is by proofreading. A large percentage of spelling errors in student writing can be traced to sloppy proofreading rather than lack of knowledge. If spelling has been a problem, you should check your paper at least once with only spelling in mind, reading your theme aloud, or perhaps improving your concentration by using a blank piece of paper to cover the sentences below the line you are reading.

Correct spelling is important, but you should not worry about it when you write the first draft of your composition, at least when you write it outside of class. As we have said, much of the frustration in writing probably stems from the fear of misspelling words, a fear that impedes the smooth flow of ideas by forcing the writer to substitute for his original word a lifeless synonym that he knows how to spell.

Your writing will probably be far more effective if you relax as much as possible, using the precise word that comes to your mind, even if you have to write it in syllables as it sounds. Later you can check your dictionary for the correct spelling. Thus a good dictionary at some stage in the writing process becomes the indispensable tool for correct spelling. If professional writers find it necessary frequently to check doubtful words in their dictionaries the inexperienced writer (especially if he has a spelling problem) must fall in love with his dictionary. Whether you check the words as you write the rough draft of your theme or wait until you have finished the first draft is up to you. We suggest the latter method so as not to block the smooth flow of your ideas. However, the ways to become a proficient speller are of secondary importance compared with your own desire and determination to improve.

Rules

Spelling rules are confusing to some students yet an invaluable help to others. Try to use them. If you find them baffling, forget them and concentrate on the individual words. Unless you understand the complete rule, you are probably better off not trying to apply it.

Composition textbooks contain many rules and their exceptions, but the following *four rules* are usually accepted as basic. They can be relied upon in most instances.

Double the Final Consonant

This rule applies to words of one syllable (like *run*) or words of more than one syllable (like *prefer*) that are accented on the last syllable. If words of this type end in a single consonant preceded by a single vowel, you should double the final consonant when adding a suffix beginning with a vowel.

Words of one syllable

bag	bagged	dim	dimmed
can	canning	grin	grinning

Words accented on the last syllable

omit	omitted	admit	admitted
control	controlling	submit	submitting

Words not accented on last syllable

benefit	benefited	profit	profiting
happen	happened		

Words That End in Silent e

If a word ends in silent *e*, drop the *e* when a suffix beginning with a vowel is added—for example, *have–having*. If a word ends in silent *e*, retain the *e* when a suffix beginning with a consonant is added—for example, *hope–hopeful*.

Suffix begins with a vowel

abide	abiding
acquire	acquired
come	coming
dine	dined
divide	dividing
leave	leaving
glare	glared

Suffix begins with a consonant

acquire	acquirement
lone	lonely
pale	paleness
profane	profanely
rare	rarely
pure	purely
purpose	purposeful

Words That Might Be Spelled ei or ie

When the two letters come after *c* always use *ei*.

ceiling	deceive
conceit	perceive
conceive	receipt
deceit	receive

When the combination follows a letter other than *c*, the sound of the syllable can usually be relied upon. If the sound is long *ee* as in piece, *i* generally comes before *e*.

achieve	niece
belief	piece
believe	priest
brief	relieve
chief	shriek

(Exceptions: either, neither, seize, leisure, financier, species)

When the sound is long *a* as in *sleigh*, *e* usually comes before *i* as in the following words:

eight	sleigh
neighbor	vein
reign	weight

Words Ending in y

In words ending in *y* preceded by a consonant, change the *y* to *i* when adding a suffix; for example, *mercy–merciful*. If the suffix begins with *i*, the *y* is retained; for example, *copy–copyist*. If the final *y* is preceded by a vowel, the *y* is retained before the suffix.

y preceded by a consonant

baby	babies	happy	happiness
copy	copies	lovely	loveliness
try	tries	modify	modifier

Suffix begins with *i*

copy	copyist

y preceded by a vowel

attorney	attorneys
chimney	chimneys
enjoy	enjoys
obey	obeyed
valley	valleys

Word List

The three hundred words that follow, particularly the ones marked by asterisks, are often misspelled by college students. More than a decade ago Dean Thomas Clark Pollock of New York University did an extensive study (*College English*, XVI, November, 1954) to determine the words most frequently misspelled by college students. After examining approximately thirty thousand misspellings, he formulated a list of one hundred words (the words designated by asterisks)[1] that cause students the most trouble. Dean Pollock's study confirmed a fact long suspected by educators: Although spelling errors frequently appear in the writing of college students, the kinds of error are relatively few. Therefore, if you will master the spelling list that follows, giving particular attention to the words marked by asterisks, you will in all likelihood solve your spelling problem and gain the confidence to write an acceptable theme.

To help you to learn these troublesome words, we have divided them into syllables, and we suggest that you concentrate on their pronunciation as well as their appearance. It might be helpful to check the words on the list that are misspelled in your themes, perhaps drawing a circle around the part of the word that caused the trouble.

There is an old proverb that says, "Wise men learn from the mistakes of others." Of course, everyone makes mistakes now and then, but the intelligent person learns from his mistakes. However, the truly wise man, as the proverb states, learns "from the mistakes of others," as you can do by learning to spell the words that follow:

[1] Reprinted with the permission of the National Council of Teachers of English and Thomas Clark Pollock.

1. accidentally	(ac-ci-den-tal-ly)	51. conquer	(con-quer)
°2. accommodate	(ac-com-mo-date)	52. conscientious	(con-sci-en-tious)
3. accompanied	(ac-com-pa-nied)	°53. conscious	(con-scious)
4. accumulate	(ac-cum-u-late)	54. consider	(con-sid-er)
°5. achievement	(a-chieve-ment)	55. continually	(con-tin-u-al-ly)
6. acquainted	(ac-quaint-ed)	°56. controversy	(con-tro-ver-sy)
°7. acquire	(ac-quire)	°57. controversial	(con-tro-ver-si-al)
8. across	(a-cross)	58. convenience	(con-ven-i-ence)
9. address	(ad-dress)	59. copies	(cop-ies)
10. advice	(ad-vice)	60. course	(course)
11. aggravate	(ag-gra-vate)	61. courteous	(cour-te-ous)
°12. all right	(all right)	62. criticism	(crit-i-cism)
13. altogether	(al-to-geth-er)	63. dealt	(dealt)
14. always	(al-ways)	64. decided	(de-cid-ed)
15. amateur	(am-a-teur)	65. decision	(de-ci-sion)
°16. among	(a-mong)	°66. define	(de-fine)
17. amount	(a-mount)	°67. definitely	(de-fi-nite-ly)
°18. apparent	(ap-par-ent)	°68. definition	(de-fi-ni-tion)
19. appearance	(ap-pear-ance)	69. dependent	(de-pen-dent)
20. appetite	(ap-pe-tite)	°70. describe	(de-scribe)
21. approaching	(ap-proach-ing)	°71. description	(de-scrip-tion)
22. appropriate	(ap-pro-pri-ate)	72. desirable	(de-sir-a-ble)
23. approximately	(ap-prox-i-mate-ly)	73. despair	(des-pair)
°24. arguing	(ar-gu-ing)	74. desperate	(des-per-ate)
°25. argument	(ar-gu-ment)	75. destroy	(de-stroy)
26. around	(a-round)	76. develop	(de-vel-op)
27. arrangement	(ar-range-ment)	77. different	(dif-fer-ent)
28. article	(ar-ti-cle)	78. dining	(din-ing)
29. athletic	(ath-let-ic)	79. disappeared	(dis-ap-peared)
30. awkward	(awk-ward)	80. disappointed	(dis-ap-point-ed)
31. before	(be-fore)	°81. disastrous	(dis-as-trous)
32. beginning	(be-gin-ning)	82. discipline	(dis-ci-pline)
°33. belief	(be-lief)	83. diseases	(dis-eas-es)
°34. believe	(be-lieve)	84. dissatisfied	(dis-sat-is-fied)
°35. beneficial	(ben-e-fi-cial)	85. divided	(di-vid-ed)
°36. benefited	(ben-e-fit-ed)	86. division	(di-vi-sion)
37. breathe	(breathe)	87. doesn't	(does-n't)
38. brilliant	(bril-li-ant)	°88. effect	(ef-fect)
39. buried	(bur-ied)	89. eighth	(eighth)
40. business	(bus-i-ness)	90. efficiency	(ef-fi-cien-cy)
41. carrying	(car-ry-ing)	91. eliminated	(e-lim-i-nat-ed)
°42. category	(cat-e-gor-y)	°92. embarrass	(em-bar-rass)
43. changeable	(change-a-ble)	93. emphasize	(em-pha-size)
44. chosen	(cho-sen)	°94. environment	(en-vi-ron-ment)
45. clothes	(clothes)	95. equipped	(e-quipped)
°46. coming	(com-ing)	96. especially	(es-pe-cial-ly)
47. committee	(com-mit-tee)	°97. exaggerate	(ex-ag-ger-ate)
°48. comparative	(com-par-a-tive)	98. excellent	(ex-cel-lent)
49. competition	(com-pe-ti-tion)	99. excitement	(ex-cite-ment)
50. conceive	(con-ceive)	100. exhausted	(ex-haust-ed)

°101.	existence	(ex-is-tence)	
°102.	existent	(ex-is-tent)	
°103.	experience	(ex-pe-ri-ence)	
°104.	explanation	(ex-pla-na-tion)	
105.	familiar	(fa-mil-i-ar)	
°106.	fascinate	(fas-ci-nate)	
107.	finally	(fi-nal-ly)	
108.	foreign	(for-eign)	
109.	formally	(for-mal-ly)	
110.	formerly	(for-mer-ly)	
111.	forty	(for-ty)	
112.	fourth	(fourth)	
113.	friend	(friend)	
114.	generally	(gen-er-al-ly)	
115.	genius	(gen-i-us)	
116.	government	(gov-ern-ment)	
117.	grammar	(gram-mar)	
118.	guard	(guard)	
119.	handle	(han-dle)	
°120.	height	(height)	
121.	hindrance	(hin-drance)	
122.	hurriedly	(hur-ried-ly)	
123.	imagination	(im-ag-i-na-tion)	
124.	immediately	(im-med-i-ate-ly)	
125.	incidentally	(in-ci-den-tal-ly)	
126.	independent	(in-de-pen-dent)	
127.	intelligence	(in-tel-li-gence)	
°128.	interest	(in-ter-est)	
129.	interfere	(in-ter-fere)	
130.	interpreted	(in-ter-pre-ted)	
131.	interrupted	(in-ter-rupt-ed)	
132.	irresistible	(ir-re-sis-ti-ble)	
°133.	its (it's)	(its—it's)	
134.	itself	(it-self)	
135.	knowledge	(knowl-edge)	
136.	laboratory	(lab-o-ra-to-ry)	
137.	laid	(laid)	
°138.	led	(led)	
139.	leisure	(lei-sure)	
140.	lightning	(light-ning)	
141.	livelihood	(live-li-hood)	
142.	loneliness	(lone-li-ness)	
°143.	lose	(lose)	
°144.	losing	(los-ing)	
145.	maintenance	(main-te-nance)	
°146.	marriage	(mar-riage)	
147.	mathematics	(math-e-mat-ics)	
148.	meant	(meant)	
149.	medicine	(med-i-cine)	
°150.	mere	(mere)	

151.	miniature	(min-i-a-ture)	
152.	minute	(min-ute)	
153.	mischievous	(mis-chie-vous)	
154.	mysterious	(mys-te-ri-ous)	
155.	naturally	(nat-ur-al-ly)	
°156.	necessary	(nec-es-sar-y)	
157.	nevertheless	(nev-er-the-less)	
158.	nickel	(nick-el)	
159.	niece	(niece)	
160.	ninety	(nine-ty)	
161.	ninth	(ninth)	
162.	noisily	(nois-i-ly)	
163.	noticeable	(no-tice-a-ble)	
164.	nowadays	(now-a-days)	
165.	obstacle	(ob-sta-cle)	
°166.	occasion	(oc-ca-sion)	
167.	occasionally	(oc-ca-sion-al-ly)	
°168.	occurred	(oc-curred)	
°169.	occurring	(oc-cur-ring)	
°170.	occurrence	(oc-cur-rence)	
171.	off	(off)	
172.	omission	(o-mis-sion)	
173.	omitted	(o-mit-ted)	
174.	operate	(op-er-ate)	
°175.	opinion	(o-pin-ion)	
176.	optimistic	(op-ti-mis-tic)	
°177.	opportunity	(op-por-tu-ni-ty)	
178.	original	(o-rig-i-nal)	
°179.	paid	(paid)	
180.	parallel	(par-al-lel)	
181.	paralyzed	(par-a-lyzed)	
182.	parliament	(par-lia-ment)	
°183.	particular	(par-tic-u-lar)	
184.	partner	(part-ner)	
185.	pastime	(pas-time)	
°186.	performance	(per-for-mance)	
187.	perhaps	(per-haps)	
188.	permissible	(per-mis-si-ble)	
189.	persistent	(per-sis-tent)	
°190.	personal	(per-son-al)	
°191.	personnel	(per-son-nel)	
192.	persuade	(per-suade)	
193.	physically	(phys-i-cal-ly)	
194.	piece	(piece)	
195.	pleasant	(pleas-ant)	
°196.	possession	(pos-ses-sion)	
°197.	possible	(pos-si-ble)	
°198.	practical	(prac-ti-cal)	
°199.	precede	(pre-cede)	
200.	preference	(pref-er-ence)	

201.	preferred	(pre-ferred)	251.	speech	(speech)
°202.	prejudice	(pre-ju-dice)	252.	stopped	(stopped)
°203.	prepare	(pre-pare)	253.	strength	(strength)
°204.	prevalent	(prev-a-lent)	254.	stretched	(stretched)
°205.	principal	(prin-ci-pal)	°255.	studying	(stud-y-ing)
°206.	principle	(prin-ci-ple)	°256.	succeed	(suc-ceed)
°207.	privilege	(priv-i-lege)	257.	successful	(suc-cess-ful)
°208.	probably	(prob-a-bly)	°258.	succession	(suc-ces-sion)
°209.	procedure	(pro-ce-dure)	259.	supersede	(su-per-sede)
°210.	proceed	(pro-ceed)	260.	suppress	(sup-press)
°211.	profession	(pro-fes-sion)	261.	surely	(sure-ly)
°212.	professor	(pro-fes-sor)	°262.	surprise	(sur-prise)
°213.	prominent	(prom-i-nent)	°263.	technique	(tech-nique)
214.	propeller	(pro-pel-ler)	264.	temperament	(tem-per-a-ment)
215.	psychology	(psy-chol-o-gy)	°265.	than	(than)
°216.	pursue	(pur-sue)	°266.	their	(their)
217.	quantity	(quan-ti-ty)	°267.	then	(then)
°218.	quiet	(qui-et)	°268.	there	(there)
219.	quite	(quite)	°269.	they're	(they're)
220.	quitting	(quit-ting)	°270.	thorough	(thor-ough)
221.	realize	(re-al-ize)	271.	together	(to-geth-er)
222.	really	(real-ly)	°272.	to (too, two)	(to, too, two)
°223.	receive	(re-ceive)	273.	tragedy	(trag-e-dy)
°224.	receiving	(re-ceiv-ing)	°274.	transferred	(trans-ferred)
225.	recognize	(rec-og-nize)	275.	tremendous	(tre-men-dous)
°226.	recommend	(rec-om-mend)	276.	tries	(tries)
°227.	referring	(re-fer-ring)	277.	truly	(tru-ly)
228.	relieve	(re-lieve)	278.	twelfth	(twelfth)
229.	religious	(re-li-gious)	279.	undoubtedly	(un-doubt-ed-ly)
°230.	repetition	(rep-e-ti-tion)	°280.	unnecessary	(un-nec-es-sar-y)
231.	resource	(re-source)	281.	until	(un-til)
232.	restaurant	(res-tau-rant)	282.	usually	(u-su-al-ly)
°233.	rhythm	(rhy-thm)	283.	valuable	(val-u-a-ble)
234.	ridiculous	(ri-dic-u-lous)	284.	varieties	(va-ri-e-ties)
235.	sacrifice	(sac-ri-fice)	285.	vegetable	(veg-e-ta-ble)
236.	safety	(safe-ty)	286.	view	(view)
237.	scarcely	(scarce-ly)	287.	vigorous	(vig-or-ous)
238.	schedule	(sched-ule)	288.	village	(vil-lage)
239.	secretary	(sec-re-tar-y)	°289.	villain	(vil-lain)
240.	seize	(seize)	290.	weather	(wea-ther)
°241.	sense	(sense)	291.	whether	(whe-ther)
°242.	separate	(sep-a-rate)	292.	whole	(whole)
°243.	separation	(sep-a-ra-tion)	293.	wholly	(whol-ly)
244.	sergeant	(ser-geant)	294.	who's	(who's)
245.	severely	(se-vere-ly)	295.	whose	(whose)
°246.	shining	(shin-ing)	°296.	woman	(wom-an)
°247.	similar	(sim-i-lar)	297.	worrying	(wor-ry-ing)
248.	sincerely	(sin-cere-ly)	°298.	write	(write)
249.	sophomore	(soph-o-more)	°299.	writing	(writ-ing)
250.	source	(source)	300.	written	(writ-ten)

G 2
H 3
I 4
J 5